# Cheese, Pears, & History

## IN A PROVERB

ARTS AND TRADITIONS OF THE TABLE

ARTS AND TRADITIONS OF THE TABLE
PERSPECTIVES ON CULINARY HISTORY

ALBERT SONNENFELD, SERIES EDITOR

*Salt: Grain of Life,*
Pierre Laszlo, translated by Mary Beth Mader

*Culture of the Fork,*
Giovanni Rebora, translated by Albert Sonnenfeld

*French Gastronomy: The History and Geography of a Passion,*
Jean-Robert Pitte, translated by Jody Gladding

*Pasta: The Story of a Universal Food,*
Silvano Serventi and Françoise Sabban,
translated by Antony Shugar

*Slow Food: The Case for Taste,*
Carlo Petrini, translated by William McCuaig

*Italian Cuisine: A Cultural History,*
Alberto Capatti and Massimo Montanari, translated by Áine O'Healy

*British Food: An Extraordinary Thousand Years of History,*
Colin Spencer

*A Revolution in Eating: How the Quest for Food Shaped America,*
James E. McWilliams

*Sacred Cow, Mad Cow: A History of Food Fears,*
Madeleine Ferrières, translated by Jody Gladding

*Molecular Gastronomy: Exploring the Science of Flavor,*
Hervé This, translated by M. B. DeBevoise

*Food Is Culture, Massimo Montanari,*
translated by Albert Sonnenfeld

*Kitchen Mysteries: Revealing the Science of Cooking,*
Hervé This, translated by Jody Gladding

*Hog and Hominy: Soul Food from Africa to America,*
Frederick Douglass Opie

*Gastropolis: Food and New York City,*
edited by Annie Hauck-Lawson and Jonathan Deutsch

*Eating History: Thirty Turning Points in the Making of American Cuisine,*
Andrew F. Smith

*The Science of the Oven,*
Hervé This, translated by Jody Gladding

*Pomodoro! A History of the Tomato in Italy,*
David Gentilcore

# Cheese, Pears, & History

## IN A PROVERB

### Massimo Montanari

TRANSLATED BY BETH ARCHER BROMBERT

COLUMBIA UNIVERSITY PRESS

NEW YORK

Columbia University Press
*Publishers Since 1893*
New York    Chichester, West Sussex

Copyright © 2008 Gius. Laterza & Figli, all rights reserved.
Published by agreement with Marco Vigevani Agenzia Letteraria.
Translation copyright © 2010 Columbia University Press
Paperback edition, 2012
All rights reserved


Library of Congress Cataloging-in-Publication Data

Montanari, Massimo, 1949–
[Formaggio con le pere. English]
Cheese, pears, and history in a proverb / Massimo Montanari ; translated
by Beth Archer Brombert.
p.  cm. — (Arts and traditions of the table : perspectives on culinary
history)
Includes bibliographical references and index.
ISBN 978-0-231-15250-1 (cloth)—ISBN 978-0-231-15251-8 (pbk.)—
ISBN 978-0-231-52693-7 (ebook)
1. Food habits—History.    2. Proverbs, Italian—History and
criticism    I. Brombert, Beth Archer.    II. Title.    III. Series.

GT2855.M6613    2010
394.1'2—dc22

2010006619

*Designed by Lisa Hamm*

# *Contents*

# Series Editor's Preface

A true and dazzling polymath, Massimo Montanari combines philology, sociological class analysis, anthropology, and cultural and gastronomic history in this delightful and readable book, fluently translated by Beth Archer Brombert.

"Do not let the peasant know how good cheese is with pears." Taking this simple unassuming proverb (and proverbs *do* constitute a collective anonymous repository of folk wisdom), Montanari shows how the antinomy of the lowly peasant food, born of lactic decomposition, and the tree-born and rare fruit, worthy of the royal table, were enmeshed in a dialectic not to be synthesized or commingled at the table by the lower classes. Peasants should remain blissfully ignorant of the gastronomic delights of cheese *with* pears!

In this eminently accessible historical narrative, Montanari traces the evolution of attitudes to cheese, that simple elemental nomadic food worthy of primitive "barbarians," the "meat of the peasantry," the saying went. Dieticians warned of a peril to health and to the digestive tract of aristocrats and peasants alike. Montanari here includes an impressive summary of medical theory from Galen to the early moderns. In the hierarchy of foods tree-grown fruits were always "socially" superior to the earthbound root vegetables and cheeses. Disdain for cheese was since time immemorial proverbially useful for the convenience and rein- forced exclusionary snobbism of the ruling classes.

Centuries later, in the courts of Europe, aristocrats who were raised indulging in the healthful and rare delicacies of the pear became gastronomes, broadening their palates into trying new tastes and hitherto neglected combinations. And so this delicious combination of cheese and pears made its way onto Italian menus, until now it seems an inevitable and decreed delicacy: "*Oncques Deus ne fist un tel mariage / Comme de poire et du fromage* [Never did God make a better marriage than the one between pear and cheese]."

For the reader of this excellent translation, it might be helpful to contrast the subject of Montanari's Italian folk proverb with an equally proverbial class distinction, dating back at least to 1393 (Gower: "Lo, how they feignen chalk for cheese"). As defined by the *Oxford English Dictionary*, this saying takes things "differing in value though in appearance not unlike." It is usually used as a sign of lack of discernment typical of an Anglo-Saxon peasant!

What is relevant here is that, unlike the more aristocratic atti- tude of the Italian proverb, cheese in England is the socially *superior* component in this antinomy. As a wise philologist stated in 1579, the proverb made black of white chalk and white of cheese. The OED is fine for tracing the philological history of chalk versus cheese; would there were a Montanari to reveal the social history behind this English elevation of cheese.

—Albert Sonnenfeld

# *Acknowledgments*

The subjects I examine in this book, along with the logic that holds them together, have fascinated me for a number of years. During that period my interlocutors, I fear, may have found the attention I devoted to them excessive. I wish to thank them for their patience, which allowed me to discuss details whose path was not always apparent. In particular, I thank my students for the stimulation they provided by expressing their perplexity and their doubt, and for proposing materials and suggestions to consider. With them I repeatedly tested the solidity (as well as the didactic benefits) of the arguments.

Francesca Pucci was of great help to me in unearthing the origins of proverbs, a subject on which she is currently working. I had many useful exchanges of ideas, too, with Yann Grappe and Nicola Perullo.

Especially affectionate thanks to Marina and Viola, who closely followed the itinerary of my research, helping me back on the road at some critical wrong turns.

*One*

# A Proverb to Decipher

---

*The tale recounted in this book has its origins in an enigmatic proverb whose meaning awaits decipherment.*

⸙

*Al contadino non far sapere quanto è buono il formaggio con le pere*: Do not let the peasant know how good cheese is with pears. This proverb is widely known in many regions of Italy with minor variations (*come è buono* for *quanto è buono*) and dialectal changes that designate one or the other subject by its local term (*cacio* for *formaggio*). My interest in this topic, which has captured my attention for some time, resides in the difficulty in deciphering the contradictory nature that appears to characterize it.

Mottos, maxims, and aphorisms arise out of meditations on the meaning of life, on the behavior suitable for this or that occasion, on solutions to pragmatic problems of survival and cohabitation. They are "help that one man offers another," writes Giuseppe Pontiggia, "a guide to avoiding error or providing a remedy for it, the comfort that experience can give someone who has not yet faced it." With regard to "authorial" advice, so abundant in the literary tradition, the characteristic of proverbial discourse is its anonymity, its presentation as "speech without a speaker" (in Michael

Camille's definition), the fruit of collective wisdom handed down anonymously and impersonally. In this way, proverbs are stratified over time to the point of becoming in the oral culture "the equivalent of *auctoritates* in the world of letters." As Piero Camporesi writes, in an illiterate world such as the peasant's, "the proverb consolidates the unattributed wisdom of the group," even if, as is not uncommon, the origin of a proverb can arise out of a signed text, reworked as a literary quotation.

Proverbs are often focused on the relations between humans, animals, weather, and seasons. Based on the "statistical calculation of probabilities," they are geared toward "the resolution of needs and practical problems," such as how to execute a piece of work in the right way, how to assure a good harvest, how to maintain good health. Equally important are reminders of duty, honesty, and moral exactitude—and also the need, at times, for cunning and self-interest—which establish and transmit "perceptions of the nature of life," as Terence Scully says. Advice and observations born of experience alternate with conventional wisdom shared by all, which lightens the discourse and facilitates communication. Equally important is the role of entertainment and socializing, assured by the irony and playfulness that are common to proverbs.

Today as in the past, food is a frequent element in the proverbial discourse. A recent collection of sayings about food, *Detti del mangiare*, lists 1,738 of them in Italy, all confirmed in present-day use in various dialectal forms. As for their existence in history, Scully has collected hundreds of alimentary proverbs from the French and English medieval traditions, organized according to a typology based on a wide variety of subjects: local cuisines, recipes, preparation of dishes; consumption of food; order and serving of meals; and so on. Metaphoric use is often made of alimentary themes: foodstuffs, cuisine, and eating are treated not only in their material dimension but also as terms of comparison in contemplating the human condition, in every figure of speech—similarities, differences, puns, ambiguities, linguistic "winks."

Nor is there any paucity of "sociological" proverbs, whose purpose is to define the status and duty of each individual, more often than not to underscore the importance of staying within one's proper place and not transgressing the limitations of one's position—proverbs that question the identity of individuals within the social order.

It is precisely within this typology that the cheese-and-pears proverb would seem to fit. But our text is decidedly anomalous within the tradition of proverbs because its prescription derives not from the desire to communicate some kind of knowledge about reality but, on the contrary, from a wish to conceal it. The declared objective is *non far sapere*, not to inform but to deny access to knowledge—and to deny it, paradoxically, to the peasant himself, in a saying that should have (and effectively does have) wide currency among the peasantry. It is all the more bizarre, then, that an admonition of "popular wisdom" that refers to the peasant (and in which the peasant is in fact the only social subject explicitly mentioned) should occur *in the absence* of the principal actor. If we were to try to dramatize this text for the theater or the screen, we would have to show a character who is speaking to another while advising, or ordering, him to keep the peasant (missing from the scene) out of their conversation.

Something is not right here. The curiosity of the historian is aroused; he wonders what the origin of such a saying can be, what it *means*, what ends it can serve.

Erasmus of Rotterdam, when he set about collecting thousands of aphorisms (*Adagia*) from the writings of ancient authors, regarded them as expressions of crystalline sagacity and absolute clarity, "clear as a gemstone." Our proverb is anything but clear, however. Erasmus himself advises us to use these brief texts, these aphorisms, these proverbs, as so many "windows on the world," useful not only to communicate moral or practical precepts in a witty and concise manner, but also to open a chink onto the historical context in which the proverb was produced—because every proverb, every text, is rooted in a specific culture, expresses it and reveals it.

My intention in these pages is to take the cheese-and-pears proverb very seriously, to treat it as a legitimate subject, and to think of it as a window on the world or as a historical document. Its very enigmatic quality may help us understand it.

# Two

## A Wedding Announcement

How did the coupling of cheese and pears occur? Documents take us back to the late Middle Ages, when the occasional pairing of the two products in the last course of a meal turned into a solid and durable marriage.

—⁂—

*Oncques Deus ne fist tel mariage*
*Comme de poire et du fromage*

Checking Google for "cheese + pears" is the fastest way to verify the presence of this combination in the gastronomic culture of today. Even if we limit ourselves to the major European languages, there are more than two million entries, with particular density in French, Italian, and English. The innumerable mentions, found in cookbooks and restaurant menus, range from commercial proposals to dietary suggestions, considerations of usage, manners of speaking. One even discovers that "in October 2007, in conformity with this ancient peasant saying" (precisely our proverb), a town in the Friuli region that is famous for its cheese production and a town in Emilia that produces pears were officially designated twin cities.

This pairing emerges as a full-fledged conscious and linguistic commonplace before becoming a gastronomic one. Or rather, it was so firmly established in the realm of food as to become an obvious mental reference and an automatic association of words.

Let us ask, then: How far back does the pairing of cheese and pears go? Are there indications or historical documents that can attribute parentage? It would seem unrelated to ancient usage. Romans ate fruit at the end of a meal, eventually accompanied by a sweet. One has to wait for the Middle Ages, in fact the late Middle Ages, before finding it associated with cheese.

The oldest evidence appears to date back to thirteenth-century France, and we find it, almost by chance, in a proverbial expression: *Oncques Deus ne fist tel mariage / Comme de poire et de from-age* (Never did God make a better marriage than the one between pears and cheese), a proverb no longer in use but still listed in the inventory of traditional French sayings.

Before we slide into an indissoluble relationship, blessed by God, moreover, we should point out that the initial pairing of cheese and pears was probably fortuitous, thanks to the occasional cohabitation of the two protagonists within the same convivial space. Both, as it happens, were preferably placed in the last phase of the meal, for reasons concerning either questions of taste or dietary science, which, in the Middle Ages, guided alimentary and gastronomic choices according to Galen's medical precepts (a subject to which we shall return). These precepts determined the techniques of cooking, the criteria of pairing, and even the order of service. One precept generally observed, even if proposed in different ways by different authors, was to begin a meal with "*aperitivi*" (from *aprire*, to open), foods that disposed the stomach to receive the foods to follow, and to conclude the meal with foods noted for their "*sigillatoria*" or sealing qualities, capable of closing the stomach so as to facilitate the digestive process. Precisely for this reason Bartolomeo Sacchi, known as il Platina, a humanist and gastronome of the fifteenth century, considered it beneficial to eat cheese at the end of the meal "because it seals the mouth of the stomach and calms the nausea caused by greasy foods." Already described a few centuries earlier by the Regimen Sanitatis of the Salerno school, this action of cheese, confirmed for centuries by dietitians, gave rise to alimentary customs still practiced today, not to mention widely known proverbs, that do not regard a meal as ended "until the mouth tastes of cheese." In this connection, we would point out, as did Jean-Louis Flandrin, that proverbial traditions often take root in premodern dietary culture, and even when the scientific bases on which they rest were lost, their practical prescriptions were conserved.

The pear was also preferably placed at the end of a meal. "You must know," wrote Aldobrandino of Siena, one of the most celebrated physicians in thirteenth-century Europe, "that all pears shrink the stomach if ingested before a meal and relax it after a meal, because being heavy, they push the food to the bottom of the stomach."

These two foodstuffs thus found themselves sharing, with diverse functions (dissolving food, sealing the stomach), the same position in the strategy of a meal. In the sixteenth century, Domenico Romoli wrote that at the end of a good drinking party (or at the end of a good meal) one should have "quince pears and cooked pears or a bit of good cheese because the sealing property of these substances soothes the mouth of the stomach." From this arose a kind of de facto conjoining of pears and cheese—encouraged and in a way imposed by convivial custom during the centuries of the late Middle Ages and early modern era—which anticipated the simultaneous serving of various foods at each course. It remained for guests to choose, according to their individual tastes, which foods to eat among the many offered together during the meal. For the last course, pears and aged cheese arrived together.

This mode of presenting courses, which provided the possibility of freely choosing one food over another, did not always result in lasting associations; often it was limited to simple alternatives dictated by personal taste. The combination cheese/pears, while in certain cases established to the point of being codified, in others continued to be accidental and, so to speak, "unhitched." This can be seen in Spain, as demonstrated by some seventeenth-century texts. In 1616 the dissertation of Sorapán de Rienos on Castilian proverbs of a medical and dietary nature claimed that cheese can be eaten at dinner as a dessert in place of fruit (*en lugar de las frutas*). Similarly, the treatise of Andrès Ferrer de Valdecebro (1620–1680) dedicated to the Why of Everything asks, "Why do cheese or pears go well together at the end of a meal?" (Note the disjunctive particle *or*.) Reply: "Because [cheese] is so heavy it falls to the bottom of the stomach and draws food there, which is where the best digestion takes place. . . . The pear has the same efficacy."

In France, on the other hand, out of occasional cohabitation arose a solid marriage, blessed by God Himself, as we are assured by the thirteenth-century proverb quoted earlier.

Another French adage places cheese and pears together, this too of medieval origin. Unlike the first, it continues to be used today: "*Entre le fromage et la poire / chacun dit sa chanson à boire*" (between the cheese and the pear each person sings his own drinking song). As explained by seventeenth- and eighteenth-century collections, this expression signifies the end of the meal when everybody starts to feel jolly and is ready to laugh," as Caillot writes. From this, in time, the first part was selected, with the terms inverted: "between pears and cheese" remained a way of referring to the relaxation that comes when the meal is nearly over, when "between cheese and pears" the conversation is most cheerful and carefree, the rapport between guests is most congenial, when, as D'Hautel's dictionary explains, one can finally "speak of a marriage"—a curious variant that recalls the idea of the pear/cheese marriage, turning it around with a kind of psychological transference onto those who enjoy these foods.

Pears and cheese in this case are simply indicators of the convivial space in which they are served and eaten. The heartier dishes have by then left the scene, and we are in the phase that modern language calls dessert. "One says *between pear and cheese* at the moment of dessert when pleasant things are said," a mid-nineteenth-century dictionary explains.

---

Even in Italy, the custom of serving cheese and pears at the end of a meal was accompanied at times by the image of well-satisfied and relaxed conviviality. The idea of amiable conversation between pear and cheese is very precisely evoked by Michelangelo Buonarroti when, in one of his poems, he described the moment at table when "*venner le frutte, il formaggio e 'l finocchio / le pere cotte con qualche sfogliata / poi quivi stetter lungamente a crocchio / a ragionar*" (there came fruit, cheese, fennel / cooked pears with some pastry / then everybody lingered to munch / to converse).

Beyond occasional contexts, it is above all the gastronomic pairing of cheese and pears that took hold in Italy with a persistence and regularity that might be considered even greater than in France (which could justify the Italian paternity attributed by many today to this alimentary custom).

Both in literary and in documentary sources, the first evidence of the pairing of cheese and pears goes back, in Italy, to the fourteenth century. The oldest attestation is perhaps in the simple verses attributed to Francesco Petrarch: "*Addio, l'è sera / Or su vengan le pera / Il casco e 'l vin di Creti*" (farewell, it is evening / now come pears/ cheese and wine from Crete).

More to the point (and botanically more informed) is the reference found in a long composition "on the nature of fruits" by Piero Cantarini, a lesser Sienese poet who lived in the fourteenth and fifteenth centuries. "Pears I bring you of every kind," writes the author: *spinose, caruelle e sementine, rogie e anche robuiole in grande schiera; sanichole, zuchaje e cianpoline, durelle e*

*vendemmiali,*[1] *el cui sapore col formaggio si ghusta* [harvest pears, whose flavor is enjoyed with cheese], *e le rugine."* Almost the recommendation of a gourmet.

Meanwhile, a valuable indication appears in notes on meals taken at the Albergo della Stella in Prato between 1395 and 1398. From this most unusual source one learns that meals often ended with cooked pears and cheese or, depending on the season, with "cheese and cherries" in May, "cheese and peaches" in September. This is priceless evidence because it concerns people of various social conditions and foods à la carte, that is, ordered by the client. There does not seem to be much difference between the alimentary practices of these hotel clients and those of Filippo Maria Visconti, duke of Milan in the first decades of the fifteenth century, who, according to his biographer Pier Candido Decembrio, liked to end a meal with "pears or apples cooked in cheese."

As can be seen from these instances, the association pear/cheese was establishing itself as a particularly felicitous variation of the widespread partnership of cheese and fruit, of which there are many amusing literary parodies, such as the one by Luigi Pulci that describes the outsized appetite of the giant Morgante and the demi-giant Margutte. They are both in a tavern and have just devoured a huge amount of meat and bread. At that point, Margutte calls over the innkeeper: "Tell me, would you have some cheese and fruit to give us, since this has not been very filling?" The innkeeper runs into the pantry and returns with an entire wheel of cheese weighing six pounds and a whole basket of apples. They are still not sated. He gathers up all the cheese and fruit he can find ("a mountain of cheese and fruit"), and the two clients make quick work of it all.

―――――⚬⚬⚬―――――

References multiply in the sixteenth century with the success of a new literary genre—comic-burlesque poetry—that is filled with allusions to objects and practices of everyday life. A master of this genre is Francesco Berni (1497–1535), whose playful *Capitoli* served as a model for a host of imitators. In these rhymes, the pair cheese/pears frequently appears. A poem by Giovanni Della Casa sings the praises of a kiss, described as tastier than anything else, including "cheese and pears." Girolamo Ruscelli, glorifying the flavor of sausage, uses as a measure of comparison the most celebrated of delicacies such as "good cheese, good autumn pears." Berni's style is reprised by Anton Francesco Grazzini, known as il Lasca (1503–1584), who in his plays launches rapid-fire allusions to our theme. In the second act of *Pinzochera* he recommends that one should always have on hand in the kitchen "*raviggioli*,[2] carovelle pears, and other fruits in season." In *Sibella* he has a scene that ends with "fruit and cheese in abundance and succulent salad."

Evidence like this is important above all for its indirect nature. It does not sing the praises of cheese and pears, but instead speaks of other subjects that nonetheless take for granted the gastronomic excellence of this pairing and refer to it as something so familiar that it needs no explanation.

In those decades, even private documents confirm that the practice of serving cheese with pears was by then established. On November 28, 1538, Francesco de la Arme, an official of the Este court in Ferrara, sent a crate of pears to the duke of Mantua, accompanied by a letter: "I am sending to Your Excellency 500 carovelle pears," to which he adds a suggestion as to how to eat the fruit: "We find them delicious with a good fat cheese from which the butter has not been removed."

Of an entirely different nature, but equally eloquent, is a comment inserted into *Natural and General History of the Western Indies* by Gonzalo Ferdinando d'Oviedo, published in Toledo in

---

[2]Raviggiolo is a small mounded fresh cheese.

1526. Translated into Italian only eight years later, it was included by Giovanni Battista Ramusio in his monumental collection *Navigation and Voyages*. Describing the vegetation of the New World, Oviedo comments on "certain trees that are called pear but do not bear pears like those in Spain. They are rather wild trees on which huge fruits the color and shape of true pears grow." At that point he stops to remark, "with cheese these pears are very good." This observation, extraneous to the phenomenon being described, is for that very reason revealing of a custom the author apparently knew well. I would not hesitate to believe that this comes from his long familiarity with Italy, where he had close relations with friends and business partners, among them Ramusio himself.

When we were seeking a starting direction for our research, in order to determine signal places and periods, the very first evidence selected decidedly led us to the where and the when. The key places seem to be France and Italy: France, where a proverb revealed to us the early awareness of the pairing cheese/pears, already attested in the thirteenth century; Italy, where this awareness appears to have gained considerable currency in successive centuries, to the point of becoming a commonplace.

Now, however, we must return to our initial proverb (*al contadino non far sapere* . . .) and ask why the tastiness of this combination should be concealed from the peasantry. Given the nature of the proverb, we will evidently have to focus the investigation on social aspects of the subject. We will do so by trying to discover what cheese and pears meant in that culture, and in those times, since a foodstuff is never a simple nutritional or dietary element but tends to define itself as having a personality of its own, endowed with a very specific "social status," in the apt expression coined by Jean-Louis Flandrin. With this as a base, we will try to find out what significance the combination of these two products could have had. Let us then begin with cheese, which, in the proverb, seems to be the principal component that brings the other component, pears, into the picture.

# Three

## Peasant Fare

---

Our proverb, however interpreted, has an obvious sociological significance. It is therefore important to establish the status of the foods in question beyond their gastronomic value. Beginning with cheese, we find ourselves face to face with the world of shepherds and peasants.

Cheese is the food of Polyphemus, the man-beast untouched by civilization. The monstrous giant, in no way like men "who eat bread," is herding his flocks when Odysseus and his shipmates enter his cave. There they find straw mats laden with cheese, and, all around, jars, bowls, and pitchers filled with milk. Odysseus rashly decides to wait for the giant in order to test his hospitality: "Let us eat the cheese and await him inside." Polyphemus storms into the cave, begins milking his ewes and goats, and immediately sets aside half the milk to curdle and later be strained through reed baskets; the other half he pours into bowls "for his supper."

This archetypal scene vividly illustrates the notion of primitive and precivilized life that cheese and dairy products long connoted in European culture. Certain "barbaric" steppe peoples are described by ancient authors—with a mixture of repugnance and amazement—as habitual consumers of dairy products: *hippomol-gói*, horse-milkers, identified by Herodotus as Scythians. Expressions such as these, which we find in authors of late antiquity and early Middle Ages, reveal a view of barbarism as a primordial state of humanity as yet incapable of controlling its own destiny, of "artificially" fabricating its own food (bread) or its own beverage (wine), a humanity dependent on nature and on the products nature "naturally" provides for humanity.

Cheese should not rightly enter into this system of values, being the product of a technology entirely ascribable to human culture. Not for nothing does Pliny the Elder take as a mark of civilization that very ability to transform milk into cheese: "It is surprising," he writes, "how certain barbaric people, though they live on milk, ignore or disdain, after so many centuries, the merits of cheese." It is nonetheless true that the image of a product is generally associated with the raw material from which it comes, in this case milk, symbol par excellence of nature and, on the level of biology, infancy. Are barbarians not the infancy of civilization?

Superimposed on the cultural prejudices of the ancient world are sociological perceptions that almost automatically associated cheese with shepherds and peasants, which is to say the food of the poor. Not always was this necessarily a negative view. Latin literature, like Greek, abounds in happy shepherds amid an idyllic, uncontaminated countryside. What does remain unchanged is the notion of *marginality*, the image of a world of poverty (or rather, the assumption thereof, based on a culturally ambiguous model of life and values) that is content with rustic unrefined food, specifically cheese.

Many important pages in ancient treatises and literature—from Cato to Varro, Columella, and Pliny—are devoted to the raising of sheep and goats and to the preparation of cheeses derived from their milk. In the majority of these texts, the consumption of dairy products is decidedly placed in a social context. Worth noting is the passage in which Columella writes that cheese "serves not only to nourish the peasant but also to grace elegant tables." The message is clear: cheese constitutes the main dish and is often the principal provision of the peasant's meal, whereas on the tables of the rich it appears as a mere "embellishment," meaning that it is not the main course of the meal or a separate course but is rather an ingredient in more complex dishes. It is precisely in this way and *only* in this way that cheese appears in the treatise *De re coquinaria* by Apicius, the only cookbook of ancient Rome that survived.

---

This ancient image recurs persistently throughout the Middle Ages. Cheese remains a sign of social and/or geographic marginality. It is the food of poor people, of pilgrims and inhabitants of alpine villages for whom dairy products are the major component of their daily diet. It is also the food of tavern clients. Cheese is a typical peasant food and the one officially provided when peasants are fed by their employers. In the thirteenth century, all peasants who were dependents of the monastery of Saints Cosma and Damiano in Brescia received a refreshment of bread and cheese when they came to the city to deliver their rental fee. But the overseer of the grape harvest received bread and meat from the owner of the vineyard. The contrast could not be sharper: cheese is the meat of the peasantry.

In a society like that of the Middle Ages, highly concerned about signaling the difference between classes and status by means of specific and rigorous alimentary customs, the lowly stature of cheese constituted a powerful, albeit theoretical, obstacle to its acceptance in the diet of the elite. This prejudice was further exacerbated by other prejudices of a hygienic and dietetic kind.

Medical science had always regarded cheese with considerable perplexity. The mysterious mechanisms of coagulation and fermentation were viewed with suspicion, and dietary treatises were invariably diffident when confronting this product, judged to be indigestible and fundamentally unhealthful. For this reason, consumption was discouraged or severely limited. It was in these terms, couched in uncertainty and contradiction, that the most illustrious authorities in the Greek and Roman wrote, echoed by European and Arab doctors of the Middle Age, that cheese if eaten only in small quantities is not noxious to the health. *"Caseus ille sanus quem dat avara manus,"* an aphorism attributed to the Salerno school of medicine, became almost a platitude in medieval medical literature and soon after assumed the status of a proverb. As of the sixteenth century we find it among Italian, French, and Spanish sayings: *Il formaggio è sano se vien dato d'avara mano*; *Tout fromage est sain s'il vient d'une chiche main*; *El queso es sano dado de avienta mano*—cheese is wholesome if served by a miserly hand. In 1583 the Bolognese doctor Baldassare Pisanelli called this "a common proverb."

According to the anthropologist Carole Counihan, cheese is a "luxury" product reserved for the upper classes, and the proverb concerning cheese and pears heard in the Florentine countryside would indicate the traditional scarcity of this food in the diet of the peasantry. This is an analysis we are already in a position to dismiss, for it is precisely in the peasantry that the social image of cheese was rooted for centuries. This cannot be the key to decoding our enigma.

*Four*

# When Rustic Food Becomes the Fashion

---

During the Middle Ages, the identity of cheese as a humble food comes under discussion and is found worthy of acceding to the patrician table.

During the Middle Ages, a laborious and not unambiguous process of ennoblement took place that progressively modified the social and cultural image of cheese. Significant in that process was the part that food played in the diet of monastic communities, which were often associated with the nobility and were well endowed with economic resources, thus anything but poor. Nonetheless, they represented themselves as poor, grafting onto the notion of "spiritual poverty"—in other words, humility—the notion of true poverty. An essential element of the monastic dietary model was the renunciation of meat, prohibited more or less rigorously by all orders. Meat was thus systematically replaced by substitute foods such as fish, eggs, or cheese. By this route, cheese acquired an importance that may have been unforeseeable. And in this way, monastic culture assumed the position of mediator between "high" and "low" dietary practices, introducing models of popular consumption into distinctly elitist social milieus. On one hand, this confirmed the status of cheese as a humble foodstuff, a substitute for another—meat, held to be vastly more prestigious and far tastier (for this reason, abstinence constituted for the monks a meritorious deprivation). On the other hand, it conferred on cheese an important position in the alimentary system.

This same culture of abstinence promoted in monastic circles thus contributed to generating new attention to cheese, for which, in time, a taste came to be acquired. "Is it possible to cite a single noteworthy cheese that is not monastic in its distant origin?" asks Leo Moulin. In reality, those "origins" are often nothing more than mythic (which, moreover, risks obscuring the fundamental contribution of the peasant world to the construction of the monastic dietary model). Myths themselves, however, are historical realities reflecting a common impression that, not entirely gratuitously, identified monastic centers as centers of the (re)development of gastronomic culture.

For the rest, the abstention from meat (and the subsequent success of "lean" foods, as they were called, which for cheese is truly a nutritional paradox) was not the exclusive privilege of monastic communities. More moderate in other periods and fashions, this type of obligation was imposed during the Middle Ages on the whole of Christendom and was observed within specific alimentary rules set by the liturgical calendar: on days of vigils and of weekday abstentions, dairy products were quickly accepted as substitutes for meat, and as of the fourteenth and fifteenth centuries they were also permitted during Lent.

This was not how the bad reputation of cheese came to an end. The ruling classes willingly did without, as we can deduce from the cookbooks (always geared to the upper classes) that appeared in Europe between the thirteenth and fourteenth centuries. If cheese was occasionally used in cooking as an ingredient in sauces and stuffings, it had a hard time getting on the table and being appreciated as a product in its own right. It was nonetheless possible to introduce certain changes. French cookbooks of this period mention cheese in fewer than one out of ten recipes. Even more "reticent" (to use Bruno Laurioux's term) was the gastronomy of the German world, while the English appear to have been downright "refractory." In Italy, however, there are signals that lead us to see a more notable presence of cheese in the taste of the elite. For example, the thirteenth-century *Libro della cucina* proposes a very simple recipe for spit-roasted cheese served to "the master" on a thin slice of bread. But it is above all in combination with pasta that cheese finds growing popularity, evidently acquiring particular popularity where pasta, in Italy primarily, becomes a foodstuff of wide consumption as of the Middle Ages. The fantasy of a land of "Bengodi"[1] is a dream typical of the popular imagination. It is a place at whose center is "a mountain entirely composed of grated parmesan," on whose summit macaroni and ravioli are cooked nonstop and then sent sliding down the slopes so that they reach the bottom well coated in cheese. Analogous to this is the comparable use of cheese in middle-class homes and in the courts of nobility.

Is it possible then to conclude, along with Laurioux, that "the taste for cheese is Mediterranean?" As it happens, the first European treatise specifically devoted to dairy products was written by an Italian doctor, Pantaleone da Confienza, professor at the University of Turin, who published a highly original *Summa lacticiniorum* in 1459. It is a veritable encyclopedia devoted to the environmental, economic, hygienic, dietary, organic, and gastronomic aspects concerning the production of milk, butter, and above all cheese, or rather cheeses, whose extensive varieties (*diversitas*) are listed for the first time, and to which thirty-two out of the forty chapters of the treatise are devoted. The author discusses the various means of producing the clotting of milk, the diverse nature of cheeses determined by the kind of milk used, the systems of salting

---

[1]*Bengodi*: *godere* means "to enjoy," and *ben*, meaning "well," is used here as an intensifier, suggesting a mythical place of great enjoyment.

and conservation, the various grades of aging. He describes and evaluates the principal cheeses of Italy, France, Germany, England, Brittany, and Flanders, most of which he claims to have sampled.

Pantaleone's *Summa* contains two noteworthy innovations. The first is a refutation of all the scientific literature preceding him when he presents for the first time a decidedly positive view of the contested product. Naturally, he does so with caution to avoid direct confrontation with the unimpeachable masters of medical science (Hippocrates and Galen) and their medieval disciples. He does this with great rhetorical ability and in perfect scholastic style, as when he discusses the affirmation made by Isaac, the great Jewish doctor of the tenth century, who wrote, "Cheese is universally [*universaliter*] unhealthful, heavy on the stomach and hard to digest." Without questioning the authority of the text under discussion, Pantaleone simply overturns the assumption, contending that the adverb *universaliter* does not comprise general validity but serves only to exclude particular cases, meaning daily use. With similar skill the Piedmontese doctor introduces a series of distinctions among types of the product and the "nature" of individuals, maintaining that there is a right kind of cheese for each kind of person. Some cheeses are suitable for older people, some for young, and each temperament requires its own kind, be it choleric, phlegmatic, melancholic, or sanguine (the four principal human "complexions" classified by traditional science). He even indicates certain uses of cheese for therapeutic purposes. The conclusion is crystal clear and unqualified: "In the final analysis, I see no reason to believe that all cheeses are to be eliminated, as advocated by some authorities, and that individuals in good health should not partake of it."

And the second great innovation: "I have seen with my own eyes," Pantaleone writes, "kings, dukes, counts, marquesses, barons, soldiers, nobles, merchants, plebeians of both sexes," willingly nourish themselves with cheese, "and so it is obvious that all of them endorse it." In that sentence lies the invalidation of a centuries-old prejudice: cheese is good for everybody—nobles and plebeians. Obviously, our distinguished doctor adds—as though to confirm an inalterable distinction—only the rich and famous (*divites et notabiles personae*) can allow themselves to follow the rules dictated by science (to choose cheese according to one's temperament, to serve it at the beginning or the end of the meal according to the grade of maturity) and to observe the "commonplace" (the oft-repeated Salerno aphorism) that recommends parsimonious consumption: "*Caesus est sanus quem dat avara manus.*" The poor, however, Pantaleone continues, "and all those who are forced by necessity into eating cheese on a daily basis, are not obliged to uphold this rule, being compelled to eat it at the beginning, in the middle, and at the end of a meal." For them at least an additional consideration is offered: "Many are so accustomed to cheese that even an excessive amount cannot harm them."

During the same period that Pantaleone published his *Summa* on dairy products, cheese achieved a degree of success in Italian intellectual circles, among humanists who, in Rome and elsewhere, while reexamining advice already proposed the previous century by Petrarch, discovered pleasure in the simple foods of the poor, borrowed from "rustic taste" (the *rusticanum gustum* praised by Gaspare da Verona). It became a genuine fashion, linked to the recovery of ancient texts and to the model of life they proposed, which was the Roman ideal of sobriety and moderation transmitted by Latin literature and ambiguously presented as "peasant" values. This new model of simplicity, essentialism, and moral rigor revived certain aspects of the monastic tradition in a new secular key, but with the same equivocations: the valorization of "the culture of the poor" from a privileged and protected social position. Typically monastic but relived in a new way, it was the practice of replacing meat with peasant foods—"of the common folk," as defined by Petrarch—such as vegetables or cheese, which were considered more wholesome.

It was in this climate that Antonio Beccadelli (1397–1471) wrote *In Praise of Cheese* (*Elogio de caseo*), in which he imagines that the cheese itself is speaking, relating how it was made by a shepherd in order to be sold in town. And in this same climate Gaspare da Verona, in his biography of Pope Paul II, praised the pontiff's refined dietary habits by specifying that he "enjoyed eating dairy products and fresh cheese at every meal."

—∞∞—

The change in attitude toward cheese, clearly perceptible in the fifteenth century, is due to the appearance during the two preceding centuries of quality cheeses, highly reputed products esteemed in the marketplace and associated with particular places of origin, as well as to particular techniques of fabrication. Pantaleone himself bears witness to this when he singles out among Italian cheeses a few excellent ones such as Florentine pecorino[2] or "marzolino" made in Tuscany and Romagna; "piacentino" (called parmesan by some), made of cow's milk in Emilia and also in the regions of Milan, Pavia, Novara, and Vercelli; and the little "robiola"[3] from Monteferrato. He then pauses to discuss the cheeses of various valleys in Piedmont and Savoy before going on to French cheeses, among which he particularly remembers craponne and brie (the latter of which must have enjoyed a degree of international renown, since it was even mentioned in fourteenth-century Italian cookbooks).

Pantaleone himself seems to have been aware of this change in the quality of the products. "Perhaps," he wrote, "the poor opinion that [Isaac, the Jewish doctor] held of cheese was because he did not like it, or had seen and tasted only inferior products, which in fact are very bad."

---

[2]Pecorino is made of ewe's milk.
[3]Robiola is made of a mix of cow's, ewe's, and goat's milk.

If in the last centuries of the Middle Ages certain cheeses began to be offered as gifts among the upper classes as a sign of worthy homage, and on occasion of self-aggrandizement (so Laurioux thinks), this indicates that the social status of cheese had indeed changed. By the fifteenth century the problem had definitively been resolved. The tortuous path of the ennoblement of cheese had reached a point of no return. In the next century, it appeared to have become solidly entrenched in the dietary habits of the upper classes, no longer as a mere ingredient in the preparation of dishes, but also as a product in its own right to be served at the table during a meal. In 1549, Cristoforo Messisbugo, writing on behalf of the duke of Ferrara, listed among the indispensable provisions in the court pantry "hard, fat cheese, tomino, pecorino, sardesco, marzolino and provature, and ravogliuoli." Bartolomeo Scappi, in 1570, reports that menus for the papal court regularly contain "splits of marzolino, Florentine raviggioli, thick slices of parmesan, cheese from the riviera, romagnolo, romanesco, caciocavallo, provature, mozzarella." Grated parmesan has in fact become de rigueur for dressing pasta, mixed—for those who can afford it—with costly spices, primarily sugar and cinnamon.

But prejudices die hard. One might even say that the very success of cheese in the high gastronomy of the fifteenth and sixteenth centuries revived the diffidence, suspicion, and polemics concerning this product with fresh intensity. Never was the discussion more alive than during that time.

# *Five*

## A Hard Road to Ennoblement

---

Heated debates and interminable polemics accompany the social ascendancy of cheese. Traditionalists resist, but it is a battle of the old guard.

The celebration of cheese is treated in the literature of the sixteenth century with much enthusiasm, even too much. The hyperbole has all the earmarks of a provocation, a challenge to the traditionalists, the old guard who continue to regard cheese as a plebeian food unsuited to gentry.

At times the echo of the dispute appears only between the lines, as in the case of the Ferrara nobleman Ercole Bentivoglio, who published in 1557 an ode in praise of cheese. After hailing cheese as the most ancient and most glorious human foodstuff ("Cheese is the first human nutriment"), the essential complement to every respectable dish ("pasta, tortelli, or meat pies without cheese cannot be . . . perfect dishes, but on the contrary, are bland, tasteless, unrewarding, dull"), and an indispensable integrator of physical energy and sexual potency ("I do not believe that a man who does not eat it can be truly vigorous"), he does not fail to observe, given these incontrovertible truths, that only fools can call it the food of the populace and the peasantry: "Blind and dumb are those who say it is a food for rustics."

In other cases the polemic is more overt and more clamorous, as in *La Formaggiata*, written by Count Guido Landi in honor of *cacio piacentino* (better known now as parmesan and made in the same province of Emilia), the star of Italian cheesemaking, which "never spoils a pasta dish" and "enhances every kind of preparation." Published precisely during those polemical years (the first edition came out in 1542), the book appeared anonymously—attributed to an improbable "Mister Stentato"—and was dedicated to cardinal Ippolito Medici, nephew of Clement VII, in whose service Landi had access to the papal court. Along with the book he sent to the cardinal was a gift of cheese: "I am sending Your Eminence a cheese from my birthplace, Piacenza." For Landi, this seems to have been a common practice. Claudio Tolomei, he too an intellectual in the service of cardinal Ippolito, thanks his friend "for the cheese you sent me." In *La Formaggiata* this practice is even recommended: "Whoever has to negotiate with people of standing . . . should offer a good cheese and immediately room is made for you and doors open."

This treatise starts out with explanations of the "material parts," meaning the substance of the cheese, whose uniqueness is the result of good pastures, fragrant grass, water, and air that contributed to its birth; the fat, healthy cows from which the milk came; and the quality of the salt that was added to it. Apart from its substance, what is perfect is its round shape (the circle is said to be the highest of all forms) as well as its extraordinary size. A cheese like that can only be "noble": "The reverend abbots, bishops, archbishops, cardinals, and popes; counts, marquises, dukes, archdukes, kings, and emperors are proud and consider it a great honor to have piacentino cheese on their table." This almost sounds like an echo of the "social" considerations made a century earlier by Pantaleone. Here the rage against the ignorant, stupid antagonists of cheese is more ferocious—Landi calls them *pecora campi*, sheep in the fields—"who generally speak ill of cheese, as though there could be anything bad about it." And why do they do this? Because, they claim, cheese is made by "gross, filthy, bestial boors," and is thus as vile as those who make it.

Landi obviously cannot deny that it is peasants who make cheese. Quite the contrary, he recognizes that "much art and skill are needed to bring this process to its completion." A certain kind of ability, a peasant know-how, deserves some manner of respect. But this does not interest Landi. Scion of the same antipeasant culture that gave rise to the prejudices he would like eliminate, he exceeds all limits of imagination (partly in jest, partly in seriousness), inventing a countryside in which the peasants become pastoral characters out of courtly operettas, having first changed their manners and even their gender. Piacentino cheese, Landi explains, is not, in fact, made by brutish, vulgar male peasants, but by "gentle shepherdesses who are pleasing and pretty," who, to begin with, draw the milk with their white hands, "sweetly singing its praises and those who produce it," then pour it into "clean, shining receptacles, which they leave to cook in large bell-shaped ovens, "well scrubbed and washed," where the milk curdles under the action of the rennet. At that point, cheese is born and the shepherdesses hasten to place it in "round molds that are bright and clean" which they begin turning. Anyone seeing them at work "with their blond braids wound around their heads," their bare arms and their skirts hiked up to their knees, their features in full sight "would be overcome by the sweetness of it all" and would willingly offer to help them with the turning. The cheese remains covered in those molds for four days, and then "the graceful, delicious shepherdesses" return to salt it, repeating this every week for a period of two weeks. At that point they oil the outside of each wheel with "charming, caressing movements" and place them in the larder. To make cheese this way "is truly a thing of lords, kings, and emperors."

Why, then, is it not appreciated by everyone? This is the same old question, no longer born of social prejudice, but of hygienic and dietary prejudices. At the heart of the polemic it is not the old guard any more who understand nothing about "the new gastronomy," but the doctors, who, with "witless and hackneyed obstinacy," continue to speak ill of cheese despite the improvement in the quality of the product. There may have been a time when it was legitimate to denigrate it because "one could not find a worthy cheese." But the old complaints have lost all validity. Hippocrates, Galen, and Avicenna were great scientists, but "things have changed today." And cheese "has been ripened and refined with time."

Landi's *Formaggiata* is a tribute to piacentino, but for us it takes on the broader scope of clearly showing us the cultural aspect of the changes taking place.

———— ✇ ————

"The witless and hackneyed obstinacy" of the doctors who refuse to admit that history marches on will continue beyond 1550. "All cheeses are bad at their core," wrote Baldassare Pisanelli in 1583, apart from those freshly made, "because as they age they get worse." In 1592 Alessandro Petronio repeats: "Every type of cheese . . . stirs up phlegm and coughing in those people who go through life without exercising, for this reason: since it cannot soften or liquefy, without great difficulty, it congeals, grows harder and remains longer in the stomach." The exercise referred to is physical, the daily labor of peasants and other workers whose robust stomachs would even digest stones ("As is known," says the peasant from Ruzante, "work can make stones digestible"). For the stomach of a peasant, cheese is just fine, but not for a gentleman's.

The decades pass, but the polemics do not abate. Quite the contrary, they become more embittered and more specific in the seventeenth century with the appearance of dissertations expressly devoted to "the noxiousness of cheese." *De casei nequitia*, the title of a treatise by Johannes Lotichius published in Frankfort in 1643, proposed for a change that the pernicious products be left "to farmers [*zappatori*, people who hoe] and proletarians."

By then it was a battle of the old guard. This is apparent from the tone of these works, conceived almost as a riposte to the ever-increasing admirers of cheese. Landi and his *Formaggiata* are the direct targets at which Alessandro Gatti aimed his *Formaggio biasmato* (cheese condemned), published in 1635 though written at the end of the preceding century, in order to maintain that "cheese has no merit, is in fact extremely unwholesome and unworthy of a reputable table."

All the arguments are familiar. "It is revolting to see animals as filthy as cows, ewes, goats, buffalo and mares, stomping night and day in their own manure, being milked by hands dirtier than the muck itself. Is it possible to find a well-born, refined person who, thinking about all that filth, can enjoy eating cheese?" Learned citations from the classics are used to demonstrate that cheese is suited only to "rustics and peasants . . . poor people and beggars . . . servants and other such low people." Absurd etymologies (*formaggio* means *fuor el meggio*, from *fuori*, outside, *il meglio*, the best, in modern spelling) alternate with puns, literary disquisitions, invectives against the *pappaformaggio*, cheese gobblers. "One should therefore stay away from any cheese," is the conclusion, and "that fool who authored *La Formaggiata* makes me laugh" with the bunch of nonsense he invented "to prove that cheese has any merit and, despite all medical advice to the contrary, is good for the health."

But the nonsense of "that fool who authored *La Formaggiata*" definitely made a breach. It is Gatti himself who lets us see that the general attitude has changed, that his point of view is now in the minority. "I do not fear the opposing multitude," he declares in the end, as though to compare his views with those of an adversary who, on the wave of a new way of looking at things, "is making every effort to defend the contrary," that is, the excellence of cheese. An "opposing multitude" had overturned the parameters of culinary taste.

# The Ideology of Difference and Strategies of Appropriation

Since people are different, they must eat in different ways. On this irrefutable axiom, alimentary customs and precepts were established during the Middle Ages and the ancien régime. However, the acceptance of humble foodstuffs for upper-class tables was accompanied by a particular strategy that modified the image, making it "socially correct."

Let us pick up the threads of our inquiry. In the last centuries of the Middle Ages, the traditional image of cheese as a vulgar, plebeian food came to be modified by a number of circumstances—its longtime promotion by monastic mores; the appearance on the market of quality products; the humanist vogue of simple rustic foods—that accounted for its admission into good society.

But that society did not believe that all men are equal. Until the French Revolution and the Declaration of the Rights of Man this remained an abstruse and incomprehensible concept. Medieval society and that of the ancien régime were entirely permeated with an ideology of difference that touched on every aspect of daily life. Literary and scientific literature continued to rehash the need to follow a diet suitable for the "quality of the person," determined not only by individual characteristics but also, and above all, by social position. To confuse the food of a peasant with that of a gentleman would endanger both the health of the individual and the social order.

Doctors had no doubts about this matter. Suitable for the stomach of the upper classes are delicate, refined foods; for that of the peasantry, coarse, heavy foods. As explained by Giacomo Albini, a fourteenth-century doctor in the service of the Prince of Savoy, to consume foods not intended for one's own rank inevitably leads to suffering and sickness. Dietary manuals, describing the nutritional benefits of foodstuffs, were careful to distinguish between those "for courtiers" and those "for plebeians," according to Michele Savonarola, a fifteenth-century physician from Padua and author of an important dietary work on *All the Things One Eats*.

For this reason, one must take more or less seriously a text, at first glance a prank, entitled *The Very Clever Wiles of Bertoldo* by Giulio Cesare Croce, which introduces into the court of King Alboino a "commoner," Bertoldo himself, presented as a hero of popular wisdom, with whom the sovereign has an ambiguous relationship, at the same time admiring and contemptuous. Published in 1606, Croce modeled his work on the medieval *Dialogue of Solomon and Marcolfo* (said to date from the tenth century), but he ended it much more dramatically: "While [Bertoldo] stayed at that court everything went from good to better. However, accustomed as he was to eating coarse foods and wild fruits, he no sooner began to enjoy those refined and exquisite dishes than he fell gravely ill to the point of death." The doctors, "not knowing his nature," sought to treat him with remedies "given to gentlemen and knights of the court," ignoring Bertoldo's supplications "to bring him a pot of beans with an onion, and turnips cooked under ashes, because he knew that such foods would make him well. But those doctors never obliged him. And so his life came to an end."

Only beans, onions, and turnips could have saved Bertoldo. The first of the "sententious sayings" he is presumed to have spoken before dying is a proverb—"He who eats turnips avoids getting into scrapes"—that was catalogued precisely at that time by Francesco Serdonati, author of the oldest anthology of Italian proverbs, who comments: "He who is accustomed to course food should not seek dishes that are too refined, for such a change could be harmful."

In short, food should sustain and nourish—in the literal sense— the identity of the one who eats it, for it not only expresses that identity but also creates it. It should moreover represent that identity in a dramatic manner. Since the upper classes are continually in search of signs that confirm and valorize the differences between the classes, the first, easiest and most immediate way of doing this is to play on culinary practices and symbols. Consequently, for a food to be considered acceptable by the gentry, appropriate strategies must be found to alter its status, thereby making it "socially correct" and compatible with the prevailing ideology. These strategies, consisting of procedures and signs, material and symbolic practices, ennoble humble foods and make their approval by the upper classes possible.

Important documentation of all this can be found in the cookbooks of the late Middle Ages and early modern era, written by court nobility or by the urban upper middle class. Recipes in those texts demonstrate the culture of the elite classes, but to our surprise, they seem to be infused with flavors and seasonings borrowed from peasant fare. Garlic, onions, and turnips, vegetables branded "rustic food" in the literature of the time, systematically appear in preparations "for gentlefolk."

And that is the point: the appearance of "lowly food" on upper-class tables was achieved with much caution and shrewdness, geared to bridging the distance between image and reality, between an ideology of difference—with which the entire culture of the period was imbued—and familiarization with the intermixing of culinary usages, as confirmed by the cookbooks.

If we think of the alimentary system as a form of language, an initial means of signaling differences, we find ourselves on a lexical level, that is, individual words, or in this case, the base product. If cheese has become a shared taste among the elite, it will not be hard to distinguish different types of cheese, some for noblemen, some for peasants. The prized brie that Italian cookbooks call for to enrich a pea soup is not merely a denomination of origin but also the exoticism of its provenance, a sign of recognition by high society. Similar praise of "the refinement of parmesan," lauded in literature in the ways already seen, went in the same direction: the choice of high quality products for lordly dining. The culture of difference is also manifest in documents that list provisions. In the court of Mantua in the fifteenth century, cheeses of various types were stocked, some for the prince's table and others for the workers who farmed his lands. In June 1458 Battista di Villanova, the farm manager, informs the Marquess Barbara Gonzaga that he has just ordered 130 *pesi*, weights, of cheese, "carefully selected and of high quality" to be sent to court, and another sixteen intended for the threshers at the farms in Luzzara and Paludano. For them, he adds, "I have ordered that they take the worst."

Other strategies of differentiation—always for the purpose of adjusting the meaning of the culinary discourse—operate on a morphological level (the enrichment of a lowly product with ingredients accessible only to the few), or a syntactical one (modification of the way a product is used, giving it another place in the order of service during a meal). An example of a morphological variant: a simple polenta with vegetables or of some other "lowly" grain can be ennobled by the addition of costly spices. An example of a syntactical variant: this same polenta can be served as a side dish with costly meat, rather than as a dish by itself. In either of these examples the foodstuff loses its "peasant" nature.

These strategies come into play in the way cheese is used. Let us recall what Columella wrote: cheese "serves not only to nourish peasants but also to grace elegant tables." This is as though to say that it is precisely the diverse syntactic role (nourish/grace) that confers diverse meanings to foods. Let us go back to what we said about cheese as the conclusion of a meal, the food that "seals" the stomach. If a food is not the meal itself (as was often the case for peasants) but is eaten only to end it, its meaning has already changed. According to this logic, the mechanism of habituation is of crucial importance, as we have seen in at least one instance: cheese added to pasta (done by everyone, peasants and noblemen alike) is ennobled by being mixed with such precious condiments as sugar and cinnamon.

At this point, a question arises: could eating *cheese* with pears not be a later practice of ennoblement?

To reply to this we have to ask: what was the social status of pears—and consequently its symbolic meaning—in the alimentary culture of the Middle Ages and the early modern era?

# Seven

## A High-Born Fruit

---

The social status of the pear, high and prestigious, is contrasted almost symmetrically with that of cheese. Which leads us to think that its combination with pears may have an ennobling effect.

Documents leave no doubt: in medieval culture, fruit was perceived as a food of the elite, even as a distinctive element of "lordly gluttony." An elegant meatless dinner described in *Erec and Enide*, written by Chrétien de Troyes in the twelfth century, consisting of first-quality fish such as pike and perch, salmon and trout, ends with "raw and cooked pears."

Delicate, perishable fruits such as pears appeared to be luxury products in a world in which the alimentation of the lower classes, always at risk of famine, was necessarily oriented to conserved or conservable foods that could provide security in times of need. In fact, even the pear, appropriately treated, could be kept for long periods. We are not speaking here of the "patrician" pear—the pear of delicate skin that ripens and deteriorates quickly, the pear that a thirteenth-century text compares to the body of a gentlewoman, instantly identifying the upper class by *its* food, whereas *other* foods (cabbage and turnips) identify the peasant. The ideology of difference rejects the commingling of the two worlds (reality is quite the opposite, as we have seen), defining as unnatural the union of a gentlewoman with a peasant, just as it would be unnatural to graft a pear onto a cabbage or a turnip.

The pear is a symbol of the ephemeral, of unessential tastes and pleasures and thus, once again, symbolic of social difference. It is therefore not surprising to find fruits, pears in particular, among the foodstuffs that the well-born exchange as elegant and distinctive gifts offered in homage as of the high Middle Ages. In the sixth century, the nobleman Vittamer, a Goth, received one hundred pears from Rurizio, bishop of Limoges, in reciprocation for a gift Vittamer had made to him, with the hope that "they do not offend his taste (*saporis gustu*)." Another hundred were intended for his wife.

The centuries pass, but the message does not change. The cultivation of fruit trees (Charlemagne himself recommended the cultivation of different varieties of pears on the royal estates) remains an economic reality of prestige throughout the Middle Ages, limited almost exclusively to upper-class lands and scarcely practiced on peasant farms. Not until the fourteenth and fifteenth centuries does one see the advance of fruit growing, stimulated by a market demand that continues to be elitist. In the meantime, the prestige of fruit becomes consolidated (as Allen Grieco demonstrated) thanks to certain philosophical and scientific theories developed in the last centuries of the Middle Ages, which postulated a close parallel between human society and natural "society," describing all living things, plants and animals, as links in a chain, the so-called chain of life, in which the value of each is determined by the position held—the higher, the more noble. Tree fruits, growing as they do above the ground, are held to be the most prestigious product of the vegetable world (just as birds, which hover in the sky, are the most prestigious in the animal world). Out of symmetry, it was felt that such foods were best suited to those who ranked high in the social hierarchy.

Precisely in this period, between the fourteenth and fifteenth centuries, the fashion of "fruit poetry" arose, a true literary genre (we have already seen one example) that testifies by its very existence to the prestige of these products among the aristocratic and upper middle classes of the time. Even the papal table bears witness to this. Various species of fruits are sought for the pantry of Paul II. As Laurioux observes, "it is the pear that offers the greatest diversity."

The custom of offering fruit as gifts retained and even increased its symbolic importance. In fifteenth-century Rome, Gianantonio Campano sent Cardinal Pietro Riario a gift of pears accompanied by an epigraph in the classical style. In 1564, one hundred pears (exactly like the gift of Rurizio—the number has an obvious paradigmatic value signifying plenty) are assembled by the "illustrious prince-bishop of Trento, Cristoforo Madruzzo," to be sent to the imperial palace in Vienna. During these same decades, the Gonzaga dukes of Mantua gain much appreciation for their custom of sending boxes of precious fruit to their aristocratic friends. Particular prestige is attached to the "*precoce di Moglia*," a type of pear that ripens early and was developed in the Gonzaga gardens.

The "fine," socially elevated image of the pear can take on erotic connotations when the exchange of gifts takes place not between lords but between lovers. Tommaso Campanella wrote a sonnet "on the occasion of a gift of pears sent to the author by his lady, which were nibbled by her teeth." The sensuality of the fruit is here related to its contact with the mouth of the lady, who mischievously bit into it before sending it to her lover. The fruit is also said to possess aphrodisiac properties: "Cherished gift between lustful lovers," the poet describes it. Curiously, this raises an unthinkable association with cheese, which was also presumed to have extraordinary invigorating powers, except as we saw in the paean to cheese by Ercole Bentivoglio, sensuality was not aroused by refined eroticism but in an impassioned and violent manner. A cultivated lordly rapture is contrasted with a brutish bestial itch.

During the sixteenth century, the theme of fruit growing gained space even in texts on agronomy and became the subject of treatises. Such is the case of *Treatise on Trees* by the Florentine Giovan Vettorio Soderini, who provides precise information about many types of pears that were known and grown in his day. A variety of pear, he starts out by saying, exists in every land, and all of them can be transplanted and acclimatized, thereby multiplying and diversifying the species. "Thus we have seen in Italy pears from Poland, Constantinople and France, the much mentioned and miraculous leaf pears . . . and the Mirandola pears whose plumpness and dimensions exceed all others . . . the bergamot pears that are called the Lord's pear, transplanted from Anatolia, and all did very well in these parts." He then goes through an exhaustive list of monthly varieties, "since in every month that follows [the month of June] it is possible to harvest not just one but many kinds of pears that mature one after the other."

Detailed instructions explain how, where, and when to plant each type, how to work the soil, how to orient the trees, how to spade and graft, how to choose the right wind, and so forth. Let us not get lost in the forest of these directions but rather restrict ourselves to emphasizing how Soderini's text makes clear the objective to pursue: how to extend the season of pears, how to multiply and diversify the varieties, not only for the purpose of varying the flavors on one's own table, but also to be able to serve them as long as possible throughout the year.

The concept will be reconsidered during the next century by Agostino Gallo, a gentleman from Brescia who wrote an important treatise on agriculture (*Twenty Days of Agriculture and the Pleasures of the Villa*) in 1569 that explains up to a point "why pears are planted rather than apples," even though they are neither as prolific nor as healthful (we will return to this later). The reason is that pear trees bear fruit year after year for a longer period, from May to November.

———⟨∞⟩———

Pears can also be dried and stored, but, as might be expected, such practices automatically rob the product of its social prestige, transforming its use and image into a function of peasant foresight, and ultimately of hunger.

During the famine that befell Italy in 1338, "people ate pears dried and ground and mixed with flour." We are informed of this by an anonymous Roman chronicler of the time. Two centuries later, an analogous usage is confirmed by a botanist from Le Marche, Costanzo Felici, according to whom "in times of need, poor people in Alpine regions, where [pears] grow abundantly, keep a large store of dried pears with which they make bread by reducing them to flour." Pears reduced to flour, to make bread no less! If this extreme practice was born of emergency, it was the conservation itself that was perceived as a choice driven by poverty. This is also noted by the Bolognese, Vincenzo Tanara, who wrote that "pears are dried in the oven, and in the sun by rustics." Not for nothing in the land of Cockaigne—"the world turned upside down" where the dreams of the frustrated peasant are made real—are pears always fresh, picked all the way into January.

A singular treatise on "rural education"—*On the Instruction of Well-Born Youth*, written in 1581 by Bernardino Carroli, a native of Ravenna—clarifies how this diversity of alimentary practices was able to transform them into signs of social position. "The fruit of the pear tree," Carroli declares, "with its many varieties and flavors, is upper class." But he advises the peasant "to plant only a few, inasmuch as it is enough to have one of each of the good ones, because these are fruits that do not keep long." In this advice, considerations of different kinds are superimposed and conflated. Pears are short-lived; therefore, it is better to cultivate only a few pear trees and to keep them for the master's table, since perishable fruit cannot (and should not) be of interest to peasants. That these fruits "do not keep well" is true only up to a point. The pear, as we have mentioned, is well adapted to conservation, a point no author fails to emphasize, separating those varieties that are best eaten fresh from those that are more "serviceable," in Soderini's words. But when pears are "declined" in this manner, they change identity. To keep them over time and transform them into a long-lasting fruit is typical of the peasant mentality. Carroli therefore prefers to ignore this. His inaccurate affirmation is a function of the upper-class image he has just bestowed on the pear.

It is specifically the pear on which horticulturists and pomologists focus their attention between the sixteenth and seventeenth centuries in their desire to please patrician taste. Jean de la Quintine, Louis XIV's horticulturist and author of the famous *Instructions for Gardeners*, published in 1690, prided himself on having selected five hundred species so that the sovereign could enjoy different kinds of pears every day. During those same years Bartolomeo Bimbi did a painting for Cosimo de'Medici III depicting 115 types of pears. Subdivided into six groups according to time of maturity (from June to winter), each species bears a number, and an illustrated catalogue lists all their names.

An absolute "infatuation with pears" (to quote Florent Quellier) spread across seventeenth-century Europe. The garden/orchard increasingly became the theater of elegance, the mark of gentility and of the refined taste that characterizes it. Affected and suggestive denominations such as Bellissima, Winter Marvel, Love's Treasure, and Jealousy accompanied the varieties and confirmed the "privileged status" that the fruit enjoyed among the elite.

This passion was justified in part by the improvement of the species and the increasing quality of the fruit. But the obverse is also true. It was this passion that encouraged the specialization of fruit growing, carrying to an extreme a culinary fancy that lasted for centuries.

Earlier we raised a question. At this point we have an answer. In medieval culture and during the ancien régime, the social status of pears was certainly high and antithetical to the status traditionally represented by cheese. The combination of the one with the other can therefore be seen as fostering a meaning of ennoblement at a time when the lowly cheese was welcomed into the privileged world of gastronomy.

One problem, however, remains unsolved: the relationship between culinary fashion and medical science. As we have seen, not only was dietary thinking harshly critical in its judgment of cheese, but it was also extremely perplexed about pears and fruit in general.

# Eight

## When Desire Conflicts with Health

Medical science was highly diffident about fruit, the object of so much enthusiasm among the elite. That was why various strategies were devised to make its consumption less harmful. The mixing of cheese and pears seems to have acquired a meaning in that light as well.

"Ripe fruit is not harmful," wrote the French doctor Nicolas Venette in 1683 in a work devoted precisely to "the use of tree fruits for maintaining good health or as treatment in the case of sickness." In Europe at the close of the seventeenth century, the passion for fruit not only corresponded to the demands of the gourmet and to the collective infatuation of the upper classes, but it could also be justified scientifically as a benefit for the health of the individual.

This was entirely new, perhaps the result of progress made in the cultivation of tree fruits and improvement in the quality of the products. Until then, medical science had remained categorically negative about fruit. And this posed a not insignificant problem from the moment that this particular food became for centuries the object of a particular upper-class desire because of its symbolic character, even before it acquired gastronomic appeal. We would do well to linger a bit on this aspect of the subject, which raises the question of how gastronomy is related to nutrition and adds new elements for consideration in our inquiry.

The contiguity of nutritional science and gastronomic practice in medieval and modern culture, at least until the seventeenth century, has been amply demonstrated in the pioneering studies of Jean-Louis Flandrin, which opened extremely fertile avenues of research. This French historian showed how the principles of medical science played a determining role in orienting alimentary choices, cooking methods, type of condiments, criteria regarding the combination and order of foods, and the modality of their presentation at the table—in short, everything that has to do with culinary practices and, ultimately, with the formation of taste. Such principles, based on the physics of Aristotle and formulated by Hippocrates in the fourth and fifth centuries BCE, were finally systemized by Galen who, in the second century CE, designed an organic and coherent scheme of analogies and correspondences between the macrocosm of nature and the microcosm of humanity. Everything was reduced to the four elements that constitute the universe (water, air, earth, and fire) and to the four cardinal humors (hot, cold, moist, and dry) with which they interrelate combining reciprocally two by two. The same combinations determine the nature of every living thing (plants, animals, humans). In the human body, the four elements and four cardinal humors are manifested in vital fluids that circulate in the organism. The different proportions of humors present in the body define the type of temperament that conditions the particular mental, material, physiological, and psychological attitudes of the individual. The sanguine is hot and moist, the choleric is hot and dry, the melancholic is cold and dry, and the phlegmatic is cold and moist. Other variables are determined by age (youth is hotter, old age colder), by gender (women are colder and moister than men) and by external factors such as climate and season.

Given these premises, it was the duty of each individual to manage his or her own temperament by moderating excesses and finding a suitable equilibrium to assure the maintenance (or the recovery) of health. This was achieved by individualizing the regimen of life (diet) to control every factor, external or internal. Special attention was given to food—considered the first among "the non-natural things (*res non naturales*)" and tied at least in principle to personal choices rather than to external conditions, which allowed a greater margin of intervention in determining an appropriate and personalized diet.

Medical opinion oscillated for a long time between the idea that diet had to be adapted to each individual according to his or her temperament (or to maintain it with foods of the same humor), and the contrary idea that it was better to contrast the temperament, balancing it with foods of the opposite humor. The first theory lasted until the late Middle Ages; then the other made its way. In each case the corrective strategy was always recommended in the event of an imbalance caused by illness (*contraria contrariis sanantur* was repeated endlessly following Hippocrates), or if the foods eaten were out of balance because of their nature.

Such was the case of many fruits that enjoyed little esteem in the eyes of doctors, being generally regarded—some more, some less—as extremely cold by virtue of their acidity. This did not prevent them from being perceived as having particular social prestige. Taste, as we know, is fostered not only by scientific considerations but also (and perhaps more commonly) by image, or one might call it fashion.

In reality pears, like all vegetable and animal products, are not endowed with a single temperament, neither by variety of the species nor by their appearance in the arc of the seasons. For that reason as well, the opinion of doctors and naturalists was often discordant. Galen described the substance of the pear as a "mixture of earth and water." Arab commentators on Aristotle in the middle centuries of the Middle Ages attributed a cold and dry temperament to the pear—"cold in the first stage and dry in the second," as described by Avicenna (980–1037), referring to Galen's classification that projected four stages of intensity for each of the four humors. This was repeated by Averroes (1126–98), though less categorically: cold and dry when green, balanced when ripe. Even more detailed is the opinion of the twelfth-century *Kitab al Agdiya*: "The elements that constitute each variety of pears are diverse. The humor of a sweet pear is hot and moist, that of a tart pear is cold and moist, and of a green pear cold and dry." He concludes, "in general it can be said that it has a certain propensity for cold."

Aldobrandino da Siena, in the thirteenth century, evokes Avicenna's judgment: "Pears are cold in the first stage, dry in the second." Aldobrandino's treatise, written in French (*Le régime du corps*, the regimen of the body) and translated into Italian at the beginning of the fourteenth century, lingers on the subject, arriving at the conclusion that it is better to avoid pears as a food and to use them only for therapeutic purposes: "In general, it is better to use them as a remedy to cure an illness than to maintain good health." This same opinion is found in the dietary compendium by Arnaldo da Villanova in the second half of the thirteenth century: "Never use them as food but only as medication." The *Tacuina sanitatis* of the fourteenth century, accompanied by illustrations of individual plants and brief dietary comments, graphically summarizes a subject already consolidated by that time: *Pira. Nature: frigide in primo, sicce in secundo* (Pear. Nature: cold in the first stage, dry in the second).

Based on these authoritative references, the same evaluation of the pear reappears in the medical texts of the fifteenth and sixteenth centuries. "Pears are cold and dry," even if "less the one than the other," and "some are more balanced," writes Michele Savonarola. In the meantime, the assertions of distrust regarding fruit continue. Castor Durante da Gualdo, author of *De bonitate et vitio alimentorum*, published in 1565 and translated into Italian in 1589 under the title *Tesoro della sanità* (Treasury of Health), reminds us that "in a regimen of good health [fruits] are unsuitable for nutrition, being of little nutritional value and generating putrid blood." If one insists on eating them, then other meticulous, detailed rules are proposed.

On this doctrinal grid alimentary prescriptions were initiated, traversing the Middle Ages and beyond. The noxiousness of pears, or in any case the difficulty of selecting among them the few edible types, discouraged their use in the daily diet. Obsessively repeated in theoretical treatises, these warnings reappeared in the advice that family doctors gave their patients, though not without disagreement. The poet/scholar Francesco Petrarch, passionate about fruit, argued politely with a doctor, Giovanni Dondi, who tried to convince him to give it up, especially since the fruit Petrarch liked—tart and not quite ripe—was held to be singularly unwholesome.

Of particular interest is the letter that Lorenzo Sassoli, personal physician of the noted merchant Francesco Datini, who lived in Prato on the fifteenth century, addressed to his patient in May 1404. The letter, entirely devoted to norms of hygiene and alimentary health, recommends parsimony in the consumption of fruit, "of which you are so fond"—yet another proof of the high esteem this food enjoyed in upper-class circles. Precisely because of this, the doctor writes, almost yielding to the evidence, "I will open my hand a bit and allow you to have almonds and hazelnuts, figs and grapes, but only before meals," as well as melon, always before meals, and ripe cherries. But that is all. Other fruits "given their harmfulness, such as beans, apples, chestnuts, pears and the like," are better left alone. Pears, absolutely not.

On the basis of such teachings, the judgments of doctors went beyond pure theory and became daily practice, conditioning and influencing the dietary choices of individuals. Highly revealing is the view of the agronomist Agostino Gallo, who, in his discussion of the moscatella pear, stresses its delicate flavor but observes, "all the same, many reject it because doctors condemn it" for the reason that no sooner picked than it rots. Once again we have the theme of perishability, the ephemeral nature of pears. The point is that this very factor, although it aroused diffidence in doctors, was one of the reasons for the social prestige of pears.

Questions of taste and fashion conflicted with those of health. Eating pears meant taking risks. To avert them helpful strategies were devised, two in particular. The first was to accompany pears with wine. "One may ask," wrote Alexander Neckham at the beginning of the thirteenth century, "how it is that pears if not accompanied by wine are harmful. Pears are heavy, hard to digest, and cold in nature. For that reason they must be taken with wine so that the heat of the wine tempers their coldness." This axiom is unambiguous and falls perfectly within the medieval framework of corrective compensations for the "humors" of foods. *Adde pyro potum*, add wine to the pear, is the aphoristic prescription formulated in the treatises of the Salerno school of medicine, because "without wine, pears are poison."

For centuries, doctors, naturalists, and gastronomes repeated this prescription to the point that it acquired proverbial forms, as happened with so many rules from that school. Numerous proverbs documented from the sixteenth and seventeenth centuries, above all in French and English, confirm this origin: *Après la poire le vin* (after a pear, wine); *Sur poyre vin boire* (drink wine with a pear); or even more dramatically, *Après la poire, prestre ou boire* (after a pear, a priest or drink). The choice is between wine and extreme unction, a proverb also found in English in the very same words: After a pear, wine or a priest.

These are proverbs that have come all the way down to today. Adolphe Chesnel and Jacques-Paul Migne, assembling in 1855 their *Dictionary of Popular Wisdom*, return to the same old medieval precepts: "If on occasion you eat a pear, you must add wine. . . . Without wine the pear is poisonous, but if the pear is a malignant fruit, then leave the pear tree to the accursed." However, beginning with the eighteenth century, these popular sayings came to be regarded as absurd prejudices. The bad reputation of pears and other fruit, which in the meantime had faded, was no longer shared by official science but remained alive in the proverbial tradition.

In Italy as well we find proverbs of this type: *Al fico l'acqua e alla pera il vino* (with figs water and with pears wine) is a saying found in various regional traditions (for example, in Tuscany and Lombardy). A variant of some interest, to which we will return, is one that substitutes a peach for a pear, without modifying the meaning of the message: "With figs water and with peaches wine," is the saying in Campania.

The second method for avoiding the danger was to temper the coldness of the pear by heating it through cooking. We still hear the rules of the Salerno school: "If you cook pears they are transformed into an antidote to their own poison." Hildegard of Bingen (twelfth century) also concurs with this in her treatise on the nature of things: "Raw they upset the stomach, cooked they make it well." Pears, she wrote, "produce in mankind bad humors when they are not cooked. . . . Therefore, whoever wants to eat pears should cook them in water, or better still, roast them over the fire." The personal choice of this German nun is to poach them, because during the cooking process water slowly absorbs the pear's unwholesome juices, whereas when roasted—because the cooking time is shorter—this is only partially achieved.

Here, too, the precept comes out of the written literature and becomes proverbial via oral transmission: *Poire bouillie sauve la vie* (cooked pear saves one's life). There is also the popular wisdom of Chesnel and Migne: "A cooked pear is an antidote, but uncooked it is just the opposite."

The image also appears in a metaphorical sense. For example, the cooked pear can also serve as a reminder of what one is doing: *Ne pas oublier la poire au feu* (don't forget the pear on the stove). Almost by definition, the pear is cooking down in the kitchen.

Even when cooked, pears are still eaten at the end of the meal. About this there is no argument. And that is why *aspettare le pere guaste* (in early Italian, *guasto* meant cooked)[1] can mean "to remain at the table until the very end" or "beyond the expected," as explained in the *Dictionary of the Accademia della Crusca*. That is how Rinaldo's impatience is expressed in Luigi Pulci's *Morgante* of 1478: "What else are we waiting for here? *Le pere guaste*?"

The two strategies are not mutually exclusive. If the pears are cooked in wine, the corrective effect is doubled. And if wine is drunk on top of that, it is tripled. Castor Durante da Gualdo, in the sixteenth century, examined all of these possibilities put together: Pears are "less harmful eaten cooked with a lot of sugar on top, along with a flavorful full-bodied wine, or actually cooked in wine, with sugar, cinnamon, or cooked must."[2]

The addition of spices during cooking is a later expedient for "heating" the product and making it more digestible. Let us remember that until the seventeenth century, digestion was compared to a cooking process (the stomach was seen as a pot) that required the right degree of heat to be properly accomplished. It is therefore not surprising that Michele Savonarola recommended that the noxiousness of pears be eliminated by cooking them with anise, sugar, cinnamon, pepper, ginger, and garlic. Other doctors of the period expressed similar views. Geremia Simeoni, in 1453, after including pears among "the enemies of the stomach," advised

---

[1]In modern Italian, *guasto* means "spoiled" or "broken."
[2]Must is the juice of grapes before fermentation.

cooking them with coriander, anise, and fennel. Giovanni Battista Fiera (1490) counseled pepper along with wine and honey.

---

Given these premises, it does not seem out of place to wonder if in this interplay of temperaments, associations, and alchemy of combinations, the pairing of cheese and pears might not also crop up. And would this not also be supported by scientific intentions, a process of correction and dietary equilibrium?

The reply at first glance is negative. No medical advice raises the question of cheese in relation to pears. The scientific road would seem to be blocked, but something suddenly reopens it overturning the terms of the argument. It is the pear that, at a certain point in our story, intervenes to correct the nature of cheese (which, as we know, was weighed down by much confusion regarding its wholesomeness in addition to social prejudice). Among the first to write about this was the Italian doctor Castor Durante da Gualdo (1565): The "unwholesomeness" of cheese can be reduced "by eating it with pears" or other fruits such as walnuts, almonds, or apples. A few years later, Baldassare Pisanelli repeats this in his *Treatise on the Nature of Food and Drink.*

These are minor intimations, unstable signals, yet they are enough to make us understand that nutrition was playing its part in the story of cheese and pears. Moreover, we can see that these texts came long after the oldest documented testimony of the mating of cheese and pears. It is as though medical rethinking intervened to justify a posteriori a usage already solidly confirmed in daily practice. This kind of scientific legitimation crowns the entire development that we have retraced. First, the "lowly" cheese is included within the universe of gastronomic privilege and pears are placed beside it, completing the process of ennoblement on a symbolic level; later, the combination is declared beneficial even on the level of health.

Naturally, the action is reciprocal. If the "cold" of the pear acts as a corrective with regard to cheese (at least the aged type, which is "hot" by nature and normally associated with pears at the end of the meal), the "heat" of the cheese operates in an equal and contrary sense. Absent from dietary texts, this second testimony appears in literature, for example, among the frequently cited verses of Ercole Bentivoglio dating from the mid-fifteenth century: "Fruits accompanied by cheese / Are less harmful, in fact healthful and good / To the taste and to the stomach more welcome / Most of all figs, and pears and melons / and peaches . . ."

We have come full circle. The social correctness of the gastronomic practice has been validated by the recognition of its dietetic suitability. The coupling of cheese and pears knows no more opposition to becoming a symbol of upper-class savoir-faire.

# *Nine*

## Peasants and Knights

---

The culture of difference is reflected in proverbs about food, which nonetheless point out ambiguous situations that are seemingly contradictory.

Our story began with a proverb. The moment has come to introduce another, documented for the first time in *Dieci tavole di proverbi* (Ten tables of proverbs), a collection of maxims in Venetian dialect, of which we have one edition dated 1535 (but there must be another going back to the beginning of the century):

> *Formaio, pero, pan, pasto da villan*
> *Formaio, pan e pero, pasto da cavaliero*
>
> Cheese, pear, bread, meal for a peasant
> Cheese, bread, pear, meal for a knight

This is a typically Italian proverb and has survived to this day. As of the sixteenth century it had already crossed the Alps, but as a proverb imported from Italy. So declares the sixteenth-century anthology of proverbs in Castilian by Hernando Nuñez de Guzman (*Formajo pero pan, pasto de vilan / formajo pan pero, pasto de caballero*), and the seventeenth-century *Dictionnaire des proverbes français*, which records only the first line ( *fromage, poire et pain, repas de vilain*), acknowledging it to be an Italian proverb.

It is essential to note that the two lines of the proverb—even if they circulate separately at times—are understood to be a single proverb subdivided into two parts. In the *Dieci tavole* of 1535, the list of proverbs is numbered, and only one number covers the two expressions. It is therefore in this context that we must seek their meaning.

At first sight, the proverb astounds us. To bring together knight and plebeian in the consumption of bread, cheese, and pears seems to recompose the social universe annulling differences and conflicts. This is how Lapucci interpreted it in his anthology of proverbs: "This is a meal as suited for people of rank as for simple folk since it is delicious but not expensive."

But such a reading is not convincing. In the society of the late Middle Ages and early modern era in which the proverb was conceived and formulated, the idea that plebeians and knights could eat the same food is (at the risk of repetition) downright impossible.

Is this, then, merely a joke, a nonsense rhyme? This cannot be excluded, but it seems hardly plausible when serious ideological themes, heavy with meaning, such as those regarding the social connotations of eating habits, come into play. It is hard to joke about a theme like that. Giulio Cesare Croce could parody it, but the parody soon ends in tragedy when his hero, Bertoldo, dies after having eaten food unsuited to a peasant.

I believe that Loux and Ricard are right when they maintain that proverbs *always* have a meaning, even when they elude us simply because the cultural coordinates within which they arose are no longer part of our mental world. Especially when the subject is food, "the proverbial discourse is detailed and precise," and most important, the relationship between the elements involved seems endowed with a meaning of great "joint coherence" even more than their individual meaning. One has only to discover it. "The essential function of the proverbial discourse is to relate, to make known the ties between elements that are habitually discrete."

Even the order in which the words and the things appear does not seem left to chance. Questions of rhyme or assonance can have their importance, but the structure of the line can hardly ever be reduced to wordplay. In the example quoted, it seems to me that it is precisely the syntax, the construction of the line and the position of the words within it that can reveal the meaning of an operation seemingly incomprehensible, like attributing to the same foods the ability to signify two social identities that are strikingly antithetical. With this in mind, I would like to propose a grammatical dismantling of the two expressions while taking into account a few fundamental loose ends that have come to light in the course of our investigation. The pair cheese + bread is certainly to be understood as one of the principle alimentary symbols of the peasant identity. The pairing of cheese and pears is probably to be understood, given the prestige of the pear, as a sign of social difference.

Let us try to understand this second plausible hypothesis, beginning with the second line of the proverb, which seems to confirm it with aphoristic evidence. Here the point of departure is provided by the pair cheese + bread (= peasant fare) to which *the pear is added*. It is this very addition that justifies the leap of meaning: the symbolic process is exactly the same as that of ennoblement, amply discussed earlier. This is why the meal is *pasto da cavaliere*, fit for a knight.

The first line, however, poses a problem. But even here the meaning does not seem inaccessible. Here the point of departure is the pair cheese + pear to which *bread is added*. When that happens, it means that the protagonist is not satisfied with this kind of snack and has to fill up: he is either hungry now or afraid of being hungry later. He therefore does not belong to the patrician world. His is the meal of a peasant. Even in literature, to eat pears and cheese "with bread" is a sign of poverty, as in a passage from *Danae*, a play by Baldassare Tacconi written at the close of the fifteenth century.

⎯∞∞⎯

The validity of this interpretation, which assigns a specific significance to the order in which the foods are presented in the text, seems to be confirmed by another Italian proverb that makes its appearance at the end of the sixteenth century in the anthology by Francesco Serdonati:

> *Noci e pane, pasto da villano*
> *Pane e noci, è pasto da spose*

> Walnuts and bread, food for peasants
> Bread and walnuts, food for newlyweds

This proverb is still heard today in Italy with an important dialectal variant that substitutes for "food for peasants" the more brutal "food for dogs": *Paen e nouç l'è un magné da spous; nouç e paen l'è un magné da caen* (bread and walnuts is food for newlyweds / walnuts and bread is food for dogs). Even in this case it is unlikely that we are faced with a play on words, a simple assonance of rhyme (moreover absent in the pair villano/spose). Too important to be lacking significance is the contrast between the two terms and between the opposing circumstances they evoke: a wedding banquet as a moment of uncommon abundance and quality of food; and the cheerless daily reality of what animals or peasants eat. Here, too, it seems possible to recognize the precise syntactical value of the parallels, suggested by the order in which the foods appear. To enrich bread with walnuts is fine dining because it signifies the transformation of daily food into a feast, as is usual for a wedding dinner (in certain regional traditions bread with walnuts is still today a symbol of a wedding). To add bread to walnuts, on the other hand, or to have walnuts and nothing else to go with bread, is the fare of hunger.

<hr />

But these nimble grammatical acrobatics run the risk of creating ambiguities and misunderstandings, which is why Francesco Serdonati isolates the second part of the proverb and proposes a reading that we did not anticipate: *Cacio, pane, e pere / Cibo da cavaliere* is merely a restatement of the line we quoted above, but he comments: "The parsimony of our ancestors is thus evident, for they respected noble persons who obligated themselves to be content with modest foods." In short, he sees cheese, bread, and pears as *modest foods*, not luxurious ones, with which knights of old nourished themselves (attested to by verses in the *Paradiso* in which Dante nostalgically evokes the uncorrupted customs in Florence in the days of his ancestor Cacciaguida).

Playing on the ambiguity of the proverbial line, Serdonati turned the terms of the argument upside down. He evidently preferred to use the proverb in order to propose other considerations that at that moment were more pressing. We are taking note of this now but will have to examine it further: with regard to proverbs, the relationship between creation and use of the text is especially dynamic. The very nature of the lines—brief, concise, schematic— carries a high quotient of uncertainty, which leaves ample room for interpretation by the one who speaks them, annotates them, uses them. This does not obviate the fact that every text has a story, sometimes an author, and a meaning one might call "original," which is what we are looking for in these pages. But every text has to confront the readings that are proposed from one time to another, and this, too, we must take into consideration.

<hr />

It was not just the subtlety of the syntactic nuances that made the proverb of the knight and the peasant difficult. The basic idea itself—that diets that appear to be similar can be substantially different—was not so readily digested and communicated. For this reason, I believe, already in the sixteenth century another version of the proverb was circulated that was more readily understood because it seemed to lack contradictions. Once again, it is Serdonati who confirms this, proposing under F for Formaggio the two separate parts of the proverb (already listed under C for Cacio):

> *Formaggio, pere e pane non è pasto da villano . . .*
> *Formaggio, pane e pere è pasto da cavaliere*
>
> Cheese, pears, and bread is not a meal for peasants . . .
> Cheese, bread, and pears is a meal for knights

The second part, however, with the insertion of the negative (*non è pasto da villano*), has overturned the meaning of the original proverb, eliminating any ambiguity and reinforcing the message, making it tautologically self-confirming: This is (not) because it is.

The new version goes back to 1611 when Orlando Pescetti published a new anthology of Italian proverbs "condensed under certain headings, and platitudes in alphabetical order." He, too, affirms that however you align them, cheese, pears, and bread are not peasant fare.

The two variants from then on live parallel lives. Giulio Cesare Croce, in 1618, preferred the older one: "*Formaggio, pere e pan, pasto da villan.*" Francesco Lena, in 1674, preferred the new one: "*Cacio, pane e pere, cibo da cavaliere. Cacio, pere e pan non è cibo da villan.*" Even today, both are in use.

Why so many variants, ambiguities, uncertainties? It will be said (and we have said it) that this is typical of proverbs. But in my opinion, there is more. Things are complicated because in this story of cheese and pears, much more than in other analogous stories, the boundaries between peasant and knight are *objectively* difficult to trace. Cheese can be gentrified, but it nevertheless remains a plebeian foodstuff. Pears can be considered a food of the elite, but it is foolhardy to think of them as an "exclusive" food.

The imaginary and the real contradict each other, in this case, even more harshly than usual. Pears (here is the problem) are not inaccessible. They are not spices, costly exotic products that alter a dish (perhaps even of peasant origin) prepared for the patrician palate. In the final analysis, it is the peasants themselves who grow pears as employees on the lands of the proprietors, or as renters or sharecroppers. It is they who on occasion sell them at the market (the peasant woman from the countryside around Imola who brings pears to sell in the city, in a fifteenth-century novella by Sabadino degli Arienti, is hardly an uncommon or strange character). In short, for pears there is a dimension of quotidian normality that collides with this exclusive image. With disarming simplicity, Piero de' Crescenzi writes that the pear tree "is a very familiar tree." And the botanist Constanzo Felici continues: "pears are widely known in all countries and on all tables."

But if the pear is a "widely known" fruit, how can the ruling classes entrust it with the delicate function of distinguishing between people, of confirming, through alimentary and gastronomic models, the ideology of difference? What is one to do if different kinds of men eat the same kinds of food? If the king eats pears and so does Bertoldo? If Bertoldo eats cheese and so does the king?

One way to avert the risks, primarily symbolic, resulting from an excessive similarity between alimentary models among knights and peasants was to introduce the idea of exclusive connoisseurship, the special ability to discriminate between cheese and cheese, pear and pear, assigning to each the products best suited to that individual. All this took place at the same time as did a fundamental change—during the very arc of centuries that we are examining—in the way the notion of taste was conceived.

# *Ten*

## To Savor (To Know) / Taste (Good Taste)

The medieval concept of taste as an instinctive form of knowledge achieved through the perception of taste was slowly replaced by a notion of "good taste"—a cultivated knowledge that could be learned and taught. Taste thus became a mark of distinction, giving rise to the idea of denying knowledge to anyone who was not socially worthy.

Is taste natural or cultural? Instinctive or acquired? During the Middle Ages, the prevalent idea was to consider it a natural capability that allowed one to know *directly* the essence of things, expressed by or emanating from their flavor. It was precisely flavor, along with the nature of the foods, that was held to be the primary means of knowing (or recognizing) their use with regard to the needs of those who ingested them, determined by the greater or lesser pleasure of their taste. Pleasure thus became the infallible guide to health, because, Avicenna said, "if the body of a man is healthy, all the things that give greater pleasure to his mouth are the ones that nourish him best." So also wrote Aldobrandino da Siena in the thirteenth century. And in the following century, the Milanese doctor Maino de' Maineri was similarly convinced that what tasted good was good for one, "since condiments make food tastier and *consequently* more digestible."

The mechanism is simple: on one hand, *need* (the physiological requirements of the one who eats) generates desire (to eat something); on the other hand, the *nature* of a food generates its flavor; if desire and flavor have a positive encounter in the process of tasting—which is to say, if the food *pleases*—then the nature of that food is suited to the physiological need of the one who eats it.

This idea is not only in medical treatises. Let us reread the lines by Ercole Bentivoglio: pears accompanied by cheese "are good to the taste, and to the stomach, more pleasing." Healthful *because* good.

With the question of taste couched in such terms, it was not possible to deny anyone—not even peasants—the ability to accede to an *instinctive* knowledge, natural, precultural, that does not arise from theory or even practice. Who teaches animals to do certain things? Montaigne ponders this in one of his *Essays*, reflecting on their ability to orient themselves, to feel, to evaluate, in short, to *know* in a noncognitive way, yet, in some cases, with greater speed and accuracy than is achieved by reason. "There must be a particular sense," Montaigne continues, "that teaches hens, before any experience, to be afraid of the sparrow hawk but not the goose or the peacock, though they are larger animals; that informs chickens of the hostility of cats, but not to fear dogs." And the following example seems made to order for us: who teaches "hornets, ants, rats always to choose the best cheese and the best pears even before tasting them?"

In short, animals at times know more than people, and what are peasants if not animals, or at best, men in a primordial state? A prototype of this human/animal species is Marcolfo, in the *Dialogo*, who is portrayed with all kinds of bestial attributes: pendulous, almost horselike lips, the rough beard of a billy goat, the face of an ass, hair like the spines of a sea urchin. His woman has long hairy eyebrows like the back of a pig, chin hair like a she-goat, asinine ears, the aspect of a snake.

These wild creatures, veritable "human animals," whose appearance reveals their animal nature, nonetheless possess a culture of their own, a kind of primordial knowledge. And in a domain such as food, the competence of the peasantry, sharpened by the needs of daily life, is incessantly confronted with the knowledge (and the demands) of the ruling classes. From this arises the need of the elite to reaffirm at all times their difference, attributing to it a "rational consciousness" which they do not recognize in the peasantry. Count Giulio Landi, in his praise of piacentino cheese, wrote, "However much the populace may recognize its goodness, not for that can they provide the reason why it is so good." Instinctively, the populace can know that a food is good, but not why.

But just a moment. This idea can be turned around. The populace may not know *why* a food is good, *but it does know it*. Herein lay the danger. The notion of taste as an instinctive capacity could threaten the system of social differences, the ideological bulwark and reassuring utopia of the ruling classes. *To the worst of pigs go the best of pears*: this devastating saying, still listed today in anthologies of Italian proverbs, seems to express the dismay of having failed to exclude the animals—and by extension the peasantry—from a taste for good things.

Medieval culture had believed the problem to be resolved by inserting—though forcing the issue somewhat—the theme of social difference into that of instinctive knowledge. As we have seen, the idea communicated by scientific, medical, and philosophic considerations was that since knowledge is instinctive and people are diverse, each person *naturally* likes different things.

This conviction prevailed well beyond the Middle Ages, and the elite classes continued to lull themselves with the idea that in any case, refined foods would not appeal to the peasant palate. His body would reject them, or would suffer the sorry end of Bertoldo, forced against his will to eat the food of courtiers.

Things got complicated, however, when the idea of instinctive taste—which opens the way to knowledge of the world and its rules—was superseded by another idea, that of good taste, meaning a cultivated knowledge filtered by the intellect.

This is not a new idea. It can also be found in medieval culture where it cohabited with instinctive knowledge (the two notions will always live side by side). It happened that, up to a point—between the sixteenth and seventeenth centuries, first in Italy and Spain, then in France and other countries—this idea of cultivated taste asserted itself and from a minority view became the dominant one in figurative usages as well. The ability to (learn how to) appreciate is not only applicable to the choice of foods—in the specific meaning of the sense of taste—but, metaphorically, to anything that makes daily life "beautiful" by filling the senses—sight, hearing, touch, smell, taste—with sensations that only an exacting, trained intellect is capable of enjoying.

According to Luca Vercelloni, all this was encouraged by the passing of the term "taste" into metaphor, no longer to indicate taste in its alimentary meaning (subjective and instinctive), but rather in its esthetic meaning—metaphor that only recently succeeded in "retroactively redefining the primitive meaning of the term, assigning a cultural quality even to taste in the palatal sense." My impression is that the notion of good taste involves, from the outset, the ability to choose food, and perhaps for that reason it was not the figurative use that gave rise to the idea of good taste but, on the contrary, the early development of this idea in the domain of gastronomy that encouraged its extension into other areas. This is the hypothesis advanced, with extreme caution, by Jean-Louis Flandrin. While admitting the possibility that "metaphoric use may have fostered . . . the appearance of good taste in things alimentary," he asks, "how could such a metaphor [that of intellectual taste] have been created and cultivated . . . by a society that was indifferent to culinary finesse and sensitive perceptions in the domain of food?" In the final analysis, it is hard to know "if the idea of good taste—or of its opposite, bad taste—first appeared in the realm of food or in the world of arts and letters." It is the first hypothesis that he finds more appealing.

One important detail: by itself, the notion of good taste in no way excludes instinct. A spontaneous, intuitive dimension is attributed even to intellectual judgment (Voltaire defined taste, in the sense of good taste, as a kind of "immediate discernment, such as that of the tongue and the palate"). But the idea of good taste that finally established itself is of a mediated knowledge, a "culturally remodeled" taste that, Vercelloni writes, matures over "a long cultural apprenticeship."

And so, it was no longer true that "what pleases is good," but "what is good is what pleases (or what one learns to like)," in other words, "good" is what is conventionally so considered by connoisseurs. The medieval adage *de gustibus non est disputandum*, which recognized the same legitimacy for all tastes determined by the natural instinct of each individual, in the modern era came up against a "progressive loss of credibility," while the idea that not all tastes have the same value and that some people more than others—so-called experts—are competent to judge gained strength. In this way, taste was defined as a "mechanism of social differentiation." Never as in the Renaissance, wrote Hauser—referring to artistic taste, but the argument has a broader range—has it been proposed to create "a culture exclusively programmed for an elite, from which the majority was to be excluded." This is the cultural mechanism that Flandrin called "distinction through taste," an idea that was long held unthinkable even if, in my opinion, it was not necessary to await the seventeenth century (as Flandrin maintains) to see it arise. In Italy, as in Spain, it could be anticipated at least a century earlier.

Two anecdotes from the life of Cosimo de'Medici, related one by Angelo Poliziano in 1477–78, the other by Tommaso Costo in 1598, illustrate the extent of the changes taking place. Both show how the subject of pears increasingly gained symbolic density in the literature of the fifteenth and sixteenth centuries.

Cosimo, Poliziano recounts in one of his *Detti piacevoli* (entertaining sayings), was giving food to a peasant and "offered him moscatella pears. But he, accustomed to big ugly wild pears, said, "Oh, we give those to pigs!" Upon which Cosimo, turning to a retainer, said, "We do not! Take these away!"

The meat of the story is this: the peasant does not appreciate delicate pears (at the time, moscatella were held in particularly high regard), because his nature is "coarse and wild," exactly like the pears he feeds to the pigs. It is almost an archetype of Croce's Bertoldo, "accustomed," as will perhaps be remembered, "to eating coarse food and wild fruit." A Catalan proverb also comes to mind, "Sire, *you* eat the pears that we throw to the pigs" (*Mon senyor, mangeu les peres, que les tinc de llançar al porc*).

Again, Cosimo de'Medici, along with his brother Lorenzo, is the protagonist of the novella written by Tommaso Costo more than a century later. The two gentlemen for their entertainment often invited a very rich peasant to dine with them. "One day at the end of the meal, they were at the fruit . . . the peasant peeled every fruit before eating it. When he did so to the moscatella pear, the two great men could no longer endure it and said to him, 'Why such zealous peeling? Don't you see you are wasting the best part?' The peasant impertinently replied, "On my lands everybody peels them, all but the pigs."

At first glance the two stories appear to be similar, but looked at carefully they reveal different attitudes toward food. In Poliziano's account the peasant is excluded by *nature* from appreciating moscatella pears, which his instinct directs him not to eat. Costo, on the contrary, describes a parvenu—the "very rich peasant"— who tries to imitate the style of living and alimentary models of the aristocracy but does so clumsily. He exaggerates his supposed refinement, which makes him look ridiculous in the eyes of his hosts who, in this instance, find it absurd to peel that particular kind of pear, thereby wasting the most delicious part. The message has therefore changed. It is not *taste* but *good taste* that differentiates people. If in Poliziano's story the master and the peasant inevitably end up eating different things, here they eat the same thing—but only the master knows the secret of how really to savor and appreciate it.

The shift from the idea of taste to good taste carries with it contradictory consequences, which Tommaso Costo's story allows us to intuit. Distancing itself from the paradigm of natural spontaneity, taste acquires a more aristocratic and elitist character. But if taste becomes a question of connoisseurs, based on the notion of learning, no one—at least in principle—can consider himself excluded from the outset. Flandrin incisively observes that while it is true that the literature of the modern era insists on the spontaneity and naturalness of "the sensations of taste," reserving it for a few elite, it is also true that "no one in these considerations of taste has advanced the idea that it could be hereditary and thus only belong to persons of noble origin."

With the new notion of good taste, the perspective has changed. The ideology of difference no longer rests on an immutable ontological given, but on the ability and capacity (aided perhaps by instinct) to learn. Evidently, this precedes the development and affirmation of bourgeois culture. But even the hypothesis that the peasant might *like* the food of the master (which would overturn the "natural" order of society) is no longer beyond the imaginable.

For this very reason it became important to negate the knowledge of anyone socially unfit to possess it. To reveal to these Bertoldos the secrets that might refine their taste and transform them into so many knights would be neither appropriate nor desirable. This concept was already expressed in the fifteenth century by Gentile Sermini with regard to the flavor of sweetness, then considered a mark of social difference: "Let the peasant not taste sweet, but sour, yes; as a rustic is, a rustic stays." In the sixteenth century this is clearly restated by Francesco Berni in a *Capitolo* that interests us particularly because it is dedicated to a fruit, the peach, which we have already seen in a proverbial saying, can play the same symbolic role as the pear.

Berni's lines, written at the beginning of the sixteenth century, define the peach as "the queen of fruits," a veritable panacea made "just for the benefit of mankind." But few knew this, only "those with taste" because peaches "contain an underlying mystery . . . that cannot be taught to crude people." This esoteric "mystery of the peach" holds the idea of an understanding that cannot be shared and *that should not be shared*, precisely so as to preserve a cultural identity (or what might be called a "sapient" identity) that consolidates and confirms class membership.

In the sixteenth century, the debate over the education of the peasantry was the order of the day. Camillo Tarello, an estate owner in the countryside of Brescia, does not fail in his *Ricordo d'agricultura* (memoir on agriculture) to emphasize that "all men naturally want knowledge." This is demonstrated by the experience of "our first relative, Adam," who, out of a desire for knowledge, did not hesitate to disobey divine law, with all the resulting misfortunes. It is therefore against nature to want to deny learning to peasants. They should, first of all, share with each other the agrarian principles in the *Ricordo*, and specifically the method—innovative for that time—for remedying the paucity of harvests by planting forage in rotation with grain crops. Beyond this precept, which will be widely accepted and exploited only two centuries later, what is notable is Tarello's insistence on the need to disseminate among the peasantry this new knowledge. "Since my *Ricordo* is to be put into practice through the intermediary of illiterate people, it seems to me that it would be very wise for the priests of every hamlet, every village, and every estate to read from it in public once a month for the benefit and intelligence of the farm workers," and to the advantage of the landowners themselves, who would profit so much more from their lands. But since the idea does not strike him as generally accepted, he presses on: "The result of being read to, though a new idea and a reasonable one, should not seem futile to anyone." To teach the peasantry was a novel idea not commonly shared—far from it. For most, the ignorance of the peasantry was quite desirable.

The terms of the debate were still heated two centuries later when Francesco Scottoni, a Franciscan, was preparing a new edition of *Ricordo d'agricultura* enhanced by his notes and illustrations. The year is 1772, and Scottoni, examining in depth Tarello's "social proposal," reexamines the necessity for providing peasants with adequate instruction and equitable contracts that will assure their cooperative effort and therefore their greater commitment to the cultivation of the lands. For this they requested long-term rentals, rather than the few years that had been the common practice. "It is not possible," Scottoni writes, "to condone a system propagated by those who, out of ignorance, want the Peasant to be poor, mistreated and ignorant." And since, he adds, to *know* substantiates *to want* and *to be able*, it will be necessary to place education alongside "the hope of changing one's condition," the will and the ability for the peasant to work his own lands efficiently. In conclusion, he says, "it is obvious that the education of the peasant is much more productive than the present system of ignorance in which others want to keep him because with their despotic ideas and maxims, they place him among things, not persons, and treat him as a fait accompli because they do not want to grant him a way out."

In short, most landowners regarded the *system of ignorance* in which peasants were held as a function of their own interests. A few far-seeing intellectuals sang outside the choir, but the culturally prevailing idea remained that of withholding education from the peasantry. Promoted in an organic and coherent form between the fourteenth and sixteenth centuries, this idea, as late as 1772, was still defined as *current*.

"Do not let the peasant know . . ." Our proverb, without any doubt, expresses that culture. It was created for the use and convenience of the ruling classes.

# Eleven

## How a Proverb Is Born

---

The birth of our proverb occurred within a cultural and economic context of aversion to the peasant world to which the ruling classes, primarily in urban Italy, denied any claim to social advancement.

At this point, all possible conditions for the birth of our proverb are present. The economic and social premises are more than evident, as are the cultural and ideological ones. The only thing missing is a formal, rhetorical invention: an archetype that in some way provides the literary model, the rhythm, the *music* of the proverb.

The archetype may be a burlesque poem by Francesco Berni, composed before August 1522, which sings the praises of cardoons—a much appreciated vegetable in Italy at the time—and expresses the hope that such pleasures remain forever unknown to the peasant.

> *Non ti faccia, villano, Iddio sapere,*
> *ciò è che tu non possa gustare*
> *cardi, carciofi, pesche, anguille e pere*

May God not let you know, peasant,
that which you cannot enjoy:
cardoons, artichokes, peaches, eels, and pears

In these three lines of the *Capitolo dei cardi* (the chapter on cardoons) is everything we have been seeking: loathing of the *villano*, the peasant; the wish that God exclude him from "knowing" (*sapere*), which would grant him the ability to savor (*gustare*) certain foods identified as a privilege of class. There is even the rhyme, *sapere/pere*. The proverb is now ripe. Its first formulation appeared at the end of the sixteenth century in the anthology by Francesco Serdonati:

> *Non possa tu mai villano sapere*
> *Cio ch'è mangiar pane, cacio e pere*

> May you never know, peasant,
> what it is to eat bread, cheese and pears

Aside from the cheese and pears, protagonists of the proverb that later took root and is still used today, Serdonati's version also includes bread. But, it should be noticed, in the same syntactic succession (bread + cheese as the starting pair with the addition of pears) as in the other proverb, documented earlier in the century, these three are identified as upper-class foods.

Serdonati's commentary on this proverb is not focused on philosophical questions of understanding or on the sensitive subject of social identity, but it raises the more concrete problem of the relation between ownership and production. Peasants should not know how good this combination is "because if it were known to peasants, they would consume even more and would cause a shortage, leaving not enough for knights." If the peasants knew, they would devour everything, and knights would suffer scarcity and want.

The economic dimension of the proverb, which had previously remained in the background, has now made a ponderous appearance on the scene. The context is by now clear.

From all evidence, the proverb of cheese and pears constitutes a gastronomic variation on the "satire of the rustic," a literary genre fairly common in the Italy of the fourteenth to sixteenth centuries, which can be defined not merely as a simple rhetorical exercise, but as an ideological instrument of the class struggle—a struggle, obviously, of landowners against peasants, geared to restraining any attempt at emancipation or social ascendance on the part of the peasants. Beyond the generic hostility toward the peasantry, the real polemical target is the newly rich peasant, the one who would presume to imitate the manners of the masters and go so far as to share their interests. The "very rich peasant" in the novella by Tomasso Costo (1596) is not up to understanding that the quality of the pear is a kind of emblem, an epigone, of the "rural elite," as Pinto calls it, which in effect was formed in the late Middle Ages and occupied economic space characteristic of the urban middle class, above all the commercial activities and in some cases the professional as well. Already then, the literature of the period had inveighed against the truculence of the parvenu.

The verses of an anonymous Genoese writer of the thirteenth century, dedicated to "the peasant ascended to prosperity," declared that there is nothing worse than "the peasant of low estate/who rises to great affluence," denaturing himself and filling himself with pride and sinfulness. It was primarily this class of the peasant world, culturally more sophisticated, that was the object of ridicule and hostility on the part of the proprietary class. Perhaps it is to this group that a variation of our proverb alludes, which, probably for reasons of rhyme, endows the peasant with the attribute "wise," knowing. The variant is in Calabrese dialect: "*Non ci diri o viddanu saggio quant'è bella la pira c'u formaggiu* (Don't tell us, o wise peasant, how good a pear is with cheese)."

Between the fifteenth and sixteenth centuries, rural society once again flattened out, the ambitions of very rich peasants were truncated, and the growing social immobility was accompanied by increasingly constricting ideological representations, which to some degree justified and supported the narrowing of privileged space. This context can explain the appearance of our proverb—a true "window on the world," as we have chosen to understand it, in the words of the great Erasmus.

———∞∞∞———

Now let us ask ourselves: is it possible to be more precise about the social identity of the counterparts who until now—following indications from sources—have been generically labeled "lords," "gentlemen," and "knights"? Let us return to the proverb of Serdonati and look for the answer there: "*Al cittadino la cortesia, al villano la villania* (To the city dweller, courtesy, to the country knave, knavery)." In Italy, the true counterpart of the rustic was the urbanite.

The "satire of the rustic," which appears in the literature of various European countries, acquired in Italy—and above all, but not only, in Tuscany—an importance unknown elsewhere. The "lord" who is contrasted with the peasant is not only, or not so much, the exemplar of traditional nobility, more interested in power than in profit from his lands, concerned with defining his way of life in terms of refinement, courtesy, *otium*/leisure. The "lord' in this case is rather the urban landowner, noble but also bourgeois, always (unlike the traditional noblemen) attentive to calculating his income, to maximizing his profit, and to exploiting most efficiently—in purely economic terms—his lands and the work of his peasants. From this perspective a previously unknown definition of *villano*/rustic emerges, no longer merely coarse, ignorant, bestial (it is above all this image that persists in the polemics on the other side of the Alps), but also a thief: the peasant who steals, the peasant as enemy of the owner's interests, hiding grain, wine, fruit. "Do you think that in harvesting fruit . . . that master has received his share?" is the rhetorical question of Bernardino Carolli in his Instructions to Well-born Youth. And in the catalogue of "Abuses and vices of peasants," compiled in 1580 by the church of Bologna on the instigation of Cardinal Paleotti, in first place is the allegation that "many feel no compunction about not giving the fair share of the harvests to the masters, under the pretext that they are too burdened by the terms [of their indenture]." Croce ironically remarks that "peasants will become accomplished thieves because by nature they are so inclined."

An allegory of extraordinarily powerful symbolism appears in a story by Sabadino degli Aretini, a Bolognese writer of the fifteenth century. It concerns a quarrel between a landowner, Lippo Ghisilieri, and a peasant, Zuco Padella,[1] an all-out war over a peach tree. What has happened is that "almost every night" the peasant sneaks into the master's orchard to steal the fruit from the tree. Lippo tries to catch him by leaving traps and spreading nails on the ground, but the peasant, though injured, does not give up. Instead, he pokes fun at the master by counterfeiting hoofprints with a horseshoe attached to his stilts to make him believe that a donkey stole the peaches. But the master does not give up, either. He has all the fruit picked except for one tree around which he orders a deep ditch to be dug "like the trap made to catch wolves." For three nights he personally mounts guard over it. The peasant returns with his stilts, goes right to the tree, and falls into the ditch, "almost breaking his neck." Alerted by the tumult, Lippo has a bucket of boiling water flung at the hapless donkey/wolf/peasant, who, at that point, reveals himself to be Zuco Padella. It will take three months before

---

[1] The name alone is derogatory—*zucca* is a squash, and *padella* is a frying pan.

he recovers from his burns, and having lost his hair, he acquires the nickname Zuco Pellato (peeled or bald). The lesson is accompanied by words of arrogant contempt: "Thieving knave that you are! You thought to fool Lippo, but he has won out over you! A thousand bloodsuckers upon you! Next time leave the fruit of my peers alone and eat your own, which are turnips, garlic, leeks, onions, and shallots with sorghum bread."[2]

The message allows no ambiguity. Tree fruits are reserved for lords ("my peers"); the peasant has no right to eat them. Foods for peasants do not grow on high branches but on the ground, or even below the ground. They are the basest of vegetables (in the order of the food chain) eaten with coarse dark bread. These and no others are the fruits intended for him.

In Sabadino degli Arienti's story the protagonist is a peach tree, but its value is the same as the pear tree. More than once have we seen how these two fruits equal one another on a symbolic level and are interchangeable for narrative purposes.

Attention should be paid to the systematic, premeditated nature of Zuco Padella's challenge to his master: *often and almost every night* he crept into the orchard to steal the fruit. The theft is not described as a sudden act of daring but a deliberate provocation of the knight by the peasant, almost as though to demand a withheld right. Even if we should avoid overloading the story with too much meaning, we cannot disregard the impression that this represents, and at the same time exorcises, an early form of the class struggle in which the peasant is not only a victim but also an active protagonist, albeit beaten and defeated. The stereotype of the peasant-thief (*colonus ergo fur*), extremely common in Italian culture of the fifteenth and sixteenth centuries, is not the obsession of the ruling class alone; from the vantage point of the peasant

---

[2]Sorghum is a coarse grain raised for fodder, but also eaten by the poor.

as well, theft constitutes the simplest manifestation—and the only one possible at the time—of the struggle against social privilege. This was noted by Giorgio Giorgetti with particular reference to the tensions between landowners and peasants in regions where sharecropping was the practice. This was confirmed by Monique Rouch, who observed how often the figure of the peasant-thief reappears in the works of Giulio Cesare Croce, whether in Italian, representing reality from the owner's viewpoint, or in Bolognese dialect directed to popular audiences. In the latter case, the peasants' "boast" is precisely to rob the masters while pulling their leg (as, for example, in *The Boast of Two Peasants, Namely the Clever Ploys of Sandron and Burtin*).

The theft of food, as noted by Florent Quellier with regard to France in the seventeenth century, came to be at times a simple "strategy for survival." But when there are fruit trees in the picture, the meaning is primarily symbolic. The gardens of the aristocracy and the bourgeoisie are besieged because to rob in that "space of good taste" that "marks the social distinction of the proprietor" is to "strike him in what is most singular about him"—a place that peasants regard with particular poignancy as the symbol of proprietary power and of their own social inferiority. Zuco Padella is a literary figure who lived, virtually, two centuries earlier, but that is already the message.

---

The extraordinary importance acquired in Italy by the economic parameters of the social contract emerges in yet another proverb in which cheese and pears are the leading actors:

> *Il villano venderà il podere*
> *per magiare cacio, pane e pere*

> The peasant will sell the farm
> to eat cheese, pears, and bread

Documented between the sixteenth and seventeenth centuries in the anthologies of proverbs by Francesco Serdonati and Orlando Pescetti, it had already appeared in a slightly different version in *La Formaggiata* by Giulio Landi, who in 1542 described it as an "ancient and true proverb" current in Milan and Bergamo:

> *Se sapesse il villano*
> *Mangiare pomi, pere, formaggio e pane*
> *Empegnaria'l gabano*
> *Per mangiar pomi, pere, formaggio e pane*

The meaning is all too clear. The peasant would ruin himself, going so far as to pawn his clothes (*gabano*) or even lose the farm, if he had knowledge of such delights. If he were to neglect his duties as a responsible farmer in order to run after the pleasures of gastronomy, it would be to his own detriment as well as, it is understood, that of his master, who would suffer a diminution of his profit. The reason being that the peasant does not know how to control himself. He is, by definition, hungry, voracious, insatiable. He is "the peasant who is never sated," of other proverbial sayings. *Importuna rusticorum voracitas*, in the words of the agronomist Piero de' Crescenzi: the voracity of the peasant is importunate.

# "Do Not Share Pears with Your Master"

## THE PROVERB AS THE SITE OF CLASS CONFLICT

A proverb is an open text whose form and meaning are determined by the varying points of view and interests of the speaker. The moral it expresses is not universal but is related to a specific connotation of class.

*You understand everything backward.*
—THE KING TO BERTOLDO

If "knights" construct (and propose that popular wisdom contemplate) a proverb that encourages the exclusion of the peasant from the pleasures of attentive and intelligent tasting, peasants on their side try to keep masters at a distance, excluding them (at least in proverbs) from their world of "ignorant" flavors.

Beginning in the fourteenth century, a meaningful proverb appeared in European literature: *Do not share pears with your master.* Do not do it, instructs a Spanish saying of the sixteenth century, "either in jest or in seriousness" (*Ni en burla ni en veras / con tu señor no partas peras*).

The reason behind this can be guessed, but there is no dearth of proverbs that explain it with total clarity. "He who shares his pears with his master does not get the best ones," says a fourteenth-century French proverb, *Celui qui partage les poires avec son seigneur n'a pas les plus belles.* The same can be seen in the traditional Italian proverb, *A chi mangia le pere col padrone non toccano le migliori* (whoever eats pears with his master does not get the best ones). A Spanish saying is even more precise: if you take the risk of dividing them with him "he will give you the hardest and will eat the ripest" (*darte ha las duras y comerse ha las maduras*). The advice, in substance, is to avoid close relations with those in power, because no matter how you do it, you lose.

With time, another interpretation arose: to choose the best pears in the presence of the master would not be impossible for the peasant but would be unfitting. Better to reserve them for the master as a sign of respect and submission: "Do not to share the pears with your master" can mean, according to a contemporary commentator, "the respect with which one should always treat superiors."

Evidently, we are dealing with "readings" explicated by the social status, which express contrasting interests. Both perspectives are present in the 1611 commentary by the English writer Randle Cotgrave on the fourteenth-century French proverb, "Whoever eats pears with his master either can not or should not select them as he wishes." In short, the meaning of a proverb, above all if it has a "social" context, changes with the changing point of view.

We will return to this shortly. In the meantime, let us look at another proverb in which the logical and narrative function of the master is taken by another character—the bear. "Whoever shares a pear with a bear always has less than half." Question: in this scene, does the bear merely play the part of the consummate glutton, or does he stand for lordly arrogance? I would not dismiss the second hypothesis in view of the frequent analogy found in medieval culture between the virtues of the *potentes*, the powerful (strength, courage, combativeness), and the nature of large wild animals such as the bear. Let us try to parallel this proverb with another that we have already considered: "To the worst pigs go the best pears." We would find ourselves before two indicators of social identity: on one side, the master represented (in the peasant's eyes) as a bear, on the other side, the peasant represented (in the master's eyes) as a pig; it is a shame that certain delicacies wind up in his unworthy stomach.

⸙

To look for the meaning of a proverb, on one side in the mental universe of the peasant, on the other side in that of the master, seems to me necessary in order to penetrate its significance, or rather the conflict of its signifiers. The two cultures intertwine and demonstrate opposing interests, but both use the proverb as an instrument to affirm its own point of view. As Camporesi remarks, from the mouths of Marcolfo and Salomone, Bertoldo and Alboino "flow the same streams of proverbs." Except that the peasant and the king use them differently and with endless ambiguities. What we hear at times is a veritable dialogue of the deaf (or those pretending to be). Thus the "wisdom" of proverbs is, at least in some cases, heavily weighted with social and cultural connotations. It is not only the context of production but also, above all, that of use that determines the meaning.

The proverb, wrote Monique Rouch, is a "polyvalent maxim" that can be adapted to various situations according to the needs and feelings of the interlocutor. It is a text that places itself in the margin of the main argument for the purpose of confirming and specifying it, while at the same time finding in it the explanatory context that the proverb, by itself, is lacking. It is *a text outside the text*, as Elizabeth Schulze-Busacker calls it, referring to the works of Greimas and Schmarje: "a prefabricated element" taken from a repertory extraneous to the text that enters it from outside, integrating it while remaining distinct. Apart from the oral or written origin, from the "popular" or "sagacious" aspect that can characterize it from one time to another, a proverb is distinguished by a particular expressive code, by a recognizable form insofar as it is "closed," which makes it possible to individuate and analyze it in the most diverse literary contexts.

The same holds true for contexts of various types such as figurative use. The art historian Michael Camille, following the intuition of Lillian Randall, thought he could trace in proverbs the origin of much of the iconography that decorates the margins of the principal illustrations in medieval codices. Andrew Otwell pointed out that this relationship is one not only of content (figures that represent proverbs) but also of function through the analogy of the part that proverbs and marginal figures play, the former in the verbal discourse, the latter in the iconographic "discourse." Marginal figures (often ironic and parodic, hard to understand by themselves) do not have a determined and objective meaning. They are allusions, suggestions to the eye that sees them, which may recognize in them a saying, a proverb, a turn of speech. Only in relation to this do they acquire meaning. Marginalia and proverbs, Otwell concludes, "are not lacking meaning . . . but they do not in themselves convey a complete meaning. They are activated by their association with a text."

This is what causes the instability of meaning characteristic of marginal images and of proverbs, which Camille defined as "speech without a speaker." And this is why the historian cannot limit himself to investigating the "origins" of a proverb, to reconstructing the processes by which a new saying enters into the collective patrimony. However valuable, such an endeavor would be incomplete if we did not try to restore to the *speech*—that is, the proverb—the voice of its *speaker*. Only the voice gives it meaning. And if the speakers are different, the meanings will be different, even if, as Schulze-Busacker has observed, whoever makes use of a proverb never reveals his personal point of view but tends, on the contrary, to depersonalize it, seeking authority in a saying that clams to be "universal" and "objective."

Ever since the Middle Ages, collections of proverbs have come down to us through a double registry of attributions, in some cases going back to ancient sages and philosophers, in others to simple folk, the populace, the peasantry. This is not necessarily a rhetorical invention. The proverbial style has long been marked either by cultivated or by popular language. However, proverbs that are identified in historical anthologies as "common," "rural," or "vulgar" can, in some instances, truly be popular in origin "even when they have been modified for use by non-peasants" so as to be "at the service of knights and officials," as Natalie Zemon Davis writes. An example of this is the collection of so-called peasant proverbs (*Li proverbes au vilain*) compiled by a twelfth-century cleric at the court of Duke Philip of Alsace, to whom it was dedicated and by whom it was probably commissioned. But the contrary also holds true. Many "popular" proverbs were in turn expressions of ideas alien to the peasant world. In the modern era, especially, many proverbs having a cultivated origin became the patrimony of a subordinate culture. The recommendation for moderation in the consumption of cheese, which Baldassare Pisanelli called "a common proverb" at the beginning of the seventeenth century, was none other than a popular restatement of an aphorism generated by the medical community of Salerno. Is "One swallow does not make a summer" not perhaps a quotation from Aristotle?

Beyond the expressive form of the proverb, what peasant culture and learned culture had in common was "the renunciation of a presumed monopoly of wisdom," as Davis puts it. *Vox populi vox Dei* was an unknown or secondary concept for a very long time. Only as of the seventeenth century did it begin to take root. Proverbs merely professed "one side of the truth," Davis remarks, but one might also say, the truth of a side.

The mechanism according to which certain rules, norms, and prescriptions entered into peasant culture, assuming a position of authority within that "popular encyclopedia" that comprised the certainties and enigmas of proverbial sayings, is a complex one that does not operate in a self-referential manner, but rather arises from the interaction of various influences, from a *circularity* of things known (already pointed out by others, in particular Carlo

Ginzburg) that demonstrates the permeability of both the culture of the ruling classes and the culture of lower classes, a continuous interchange between high and low in the definition of learning models.

The circularity of models, which did not exclude deep contrasts and conflicts, seems to have diminished in the eighteenth century when the Enlightenment railed against proverbs as a "den" of superstition and "popular misconceptions" to be fought in the name of science. But the very same ideal of educating the populace (to combat medical prejudices, or to promote new farming methods) made use of the proverb as a medium of communication and propaganda. One need only leaf through texts on agronomy to discover a way of thinking literally stuffed with proverbial phraseology. Also revealing, and explicit in its complexity, is the circular mechanism referred to earlier.

The best example, it seems to me, is a brief work, one of many by Provost Marco Lastri, a highly active promoter of agronomy in the Tuscan countryside during the last years of the eighteenth century, titled *Proverbs for peasants divided into four categories, to serve as precepts for agriculture: a handbook intended for landowners to circulate among their peasants, who in turn will acquire useful knowledge for increasing annual harvests.* Published in 1790 in Venice (but the proverbs were already in an earlier edition of the *Treatise on Agriculture* by the same author), the handbook illustrates by its title alone the cultural significance of the endeavor: Lastri, the intellectual, collects, but also *produces* proverbs, diffusing them among the landowners to make them known to the peasants who accept them as rules of conduct.

So long as the subject of proverbs was information about climate and the seasons or instructions on the labors to be accomplished in this or that month, it is hardly surprising that the peasant tradition adopted them as its own, although in some cases peasants themselves may have been at the origin of this tradition; after all, the observation of nature and its vital cycles is certainly not the sole prerogative of landowners. Less obvious is that peasants welcomed into their own repertory of proverbs an adage such as the one about cheese and pears, inspired by a cruel antipeasant satire that, in its original meaning, hoped for the exclusion of rustics from the secrets of gastronomy. And yet, even this adage came into use and was documented in the collection of "popular sayings," as defined by Giuseppe Giusti in 1853 in the introduction to his *Tuscan Proverbs*. It is precisely Giusti's collection, enlarged in 1871 by Gino Capponi, that provides the principal link connecting the proverbial tradition of the sixteenth century with the anthologies that still today list our proverb, which has remained solidly entrenched in the spoken language.

The fact is that proverbs are extratextual and have a life of their own outside of the texts waiting to be activated and to acquire a meaning. Having become popular, the proverb of cheese and pears awaited a (new) meaning, coherent with the (new) text it accompanied, that is, the text of peasant speech, discourse that is spoken and handed down orally.

When it is not reduced to a kind of insignificant nursery rhyme (many today, when asked about the meaning of the proverb under discussion, admit they do not know), the proverb assumes an ironic quality that pokes fun at the original meaning and with a sly wink attributes to the imperative *do not let know* the meaning of "it is unnecessary, it is superfluous to let know." Amply confirmed in oral use, this decisive variant of meaning (probably after the nineteenth century) also appears in the commentary that accompanies the most recent anthologies of proverbial locutions. "Why conceal this delectable secret from peasants?" Dino Provenzal asks. "Because they are not considered worthy of such exquisite pleasures? Because they would devour all the master's cheese and pears? Mystery. What is certain is that the contemptuous phrase is widely known." The first hypothesis (because they already know) was unquestioningly accepted by Bruna Lancia in the introduction to the previously mentioned *Detti del mangiare* (sayings about food): "The coupling of cheese and pears is so delicious that it needs no publicity for the peasant, who produces both of them."

In this way the meaning of the proverb has been literally subverted: once the speaker has changed, the speech acquires another meaning. The peasantry, after having appropriated an adage invented *against them*, has turned the satire *against the opponent*. A new proverb could even be coined, the equal and contrary of the preceding one, in which the repository of wisdom is not the master, but the peasant: *Al padrone non far sapere / quanto è buono il formaggio con le pere.*

The cultural mechanism that generates this mutation is manifested in the extended version of the proverb, vengeful and liberating, still heard today in the countryside around Siena:

> *Al contadino non far sapere*
> *Quanto è buono il formaggio con le pere.*
> *Ma il contadino, che non era coglione,*
> *Lo sapeva prima del padrone.*

> Do not let the peasant know
> How good is cheese with pears.
> But the peasant, who was no jerk,
> Knew it before the master.

# References

*"May God curse you, Sancho," Don Quixote said at that point.
"May sixty thousand devils take you and your proverbs away!"*

## Chapter 1. A Proverb to Decipher

Listings of the proverb in some recent anthologies and dictionaries: *I detti del mangiare: 1738 proverbi segnalati da 1853 medici commentati in chiave nutrizionale da Bruna Lancia*, ed. L. Antoniazzi and L. Citti (Milan: Editemme, 1988), p. 22. (The proverb is listed as nos. 7, 94, and 1225 in the Abruzzese, Calabrese, and Tuscan regional variants.)

P. Guazzotti and M. F. Oddera, *Il grande dizionario dei proverbi italiani* (Bologna: Zanichelli, 2006), p. 37; C. Lapucci, *Dizionario dei proverbi italiani* (Milan: Mondadori, 2007), C 2101, p. 358.

For the other citations: G. Pontiggia, preface to *Scrittori italiani di aforismi*, ed. G. Ruozzi (Milan: Mondadori, 1994), p. 27; M. Camille, *Image on the Edge: Margins of Medieval Art* (Cambridge, Mass.: Harvard University Press, 1992), p. 36; P. Camporesi, "La formazione e la trasmissione del sapere nelle società pastorali e contadine," *Estudis d'historia agrària* V (1985), pp. 77–89; T. Scully, "*Comme lard es pois*: Middle-French Proverbs with Reference to Food," *Petits Propos Culinaires* 82 (2006), pp. 17–35 (on p. 17 of which I provide the list of proverbs).

The quotation from Erasmus is taken from N. Zemon Davis, *Le culture del popolo. Sapere, rituali e resistenze nella Francia del Cinquecento* (Turin: Einaudi, 1980), p. 316.

# Chapter 2. A Wedding Announcement

Notice of the curious twinning is taken from www.freshplaza.it/news (26/11/2007).

On Roman culinary customs, see F. Dupont, "Grammatica dell'alimentazione e dei pasti romani," in *Storia dell'alimentazione*, ed. J.-L. Flandrin and M. Montanari (Rome: Laterza, 1997), p. 157; A. Dosi and F. Schnell, *A tavola con i romani antichi* (Rome: Quasar, 1984), p. 63.

The thirteenth-century French proverb is in J. Morawski, *Proverbes français antérieurs au XV siècle*, n. 1443 (Paris: Champion, 1925). It is also cited by J.-L. Flandrin, *Alimentation et médecine, Histoire de l'alimentation occidentale: diététiques ancienne et formation du goût. Proverbes diététiques*, n. 3 (see article on www.mangeur-ocha.com). For its continuation today, see G. Cosson, *Inventaire des dictons des terroirs de France* (Paris: Larousse, 2006), p. 146. An abbreviated form (*La poire avec le fromage, c'est mariage*) is in the nineteenth-century anthology by A. Chesnel and J.-P. Migne, *Dictionnaire de la sagesse populaire, recueil moral d'apophthegmes, axiomes, etc.* (1855), p. 803 n. 109.

On the influence of Galenic medicine on gastronomic choices and order of service, see A. Capatti and M. Montanari, *La cucina italiana. Storia di una cultura* (Rome: Laterza, 1999), pp. 145 ff. (*Il cuoco galenico*). The medieval and Renaissance system of "simultaneous" service ended in Europe only in the nineteenth century with the establishment of the "Russian-style service" currently in practice, in which "all dishes are presented to each individual guest in a pre-determined succession" (ibid., p. 171).

On Platina and the culture of his time, see B. Laurioux, *Gastronomie, humanisme et société à Rome au milieu du XV^e siècle. Autour de "De honesta voluptate" de Platina* (Florence: Sismel/Edizioni del Galluzzo, 2006). The citation is from *De honesta voluptate et valetudine*, which I use in its Italian translation: B. Platina, *Il Piacere onesto e la buona salute*, ed. E. Faccioli (Turin: Einaudi, 1985, p. 51). For the aphorism from the Salerno school: *Regimen Sanitatis, Flos medicinae Scholae Salerni*, ed. A. Sinno (Milan: Mursia, 1987), I, IX, 8, p. 122: "*si post sumatur, terminet ille dapes*" (if one eats cheese after other foods, the meal can be considered ended). For the proverbs resulting from the medieval "rule," I have quoted from V. Boggione and L. Massobrio, *Dizionario dei proverbi. I proverbi italiani organizzati per temi* (Turin: Utet, 2004), V.1.7.8.21–22. Other examples are in C. Lapucci, *Dizionario dei proverbi italiani*, F 1081: "*Non si alza da tavola se la bocca non sa di formaggio*" (One does not rise from the table without the taste of cheese in the mouth); P 2439: "*Il pranzo non vale un'acca se non finisce col gusto di vacca*" (the meal is not worth a damn if it does not end with the taste of cow); P 1440: "*La bocca*

*non è stracca se non sa di vacca"* (the mouth is not sated if it does not taste of cow); Antoniazzi and Citti, *I detti del mangiare*, 375 (Friuli), 611 (Lombardy), 790 (Piedmont). It should be noted that at least in one case cheese is paired with fruit: "*Da teula n'talver mai sa le to boca la 'n sa ed fruta o 'd furmaj*" (Do not rise from the table if your mouth does not taste of fruit or cheese), Emilian proverb, ibid, 309.

J.-L. Flandrin has studied in depth the relationship in varying circumstances between proverbs and premodern dietetics: in particular, see "Condimenti, cucina e dietetica tra XIV e XVI secolo," in *Storia dell'alimentazione*, pp. 392–394, on diet and oral culture.

For the quotation from Aldobrandino, see Aldebrandin de Sienne, *Le régime du corps*, ed. L. Landouzy and R. Pépin (Paris: Champion, 1911; Geneva: Slatkine, 1978), p. 147: "*Sachiez que toutes poires estraignent le ventrail devant mangier, et apriès mangier l'alaschent; por ce qu'eles sont pesans, si font le viande avaler*." Translation in text.

The text by Romoli is quoted in *Grande dizionario della lingua italiana* (Turin: Utet, 1961), "Pera."

The two Spanish texts quoted are J. Sorapàn de Rieros, *Medicina española contenida en proverbios vulgares de nuestra lengua* (Granada, 1616), 1, p. 250 (cf. J. Cruz Cruz, *Dietetica medieval* [Huesca: La Val de Onera, 1997], p. 215); A. Ferrer de Valdecebro, *Il perché di tutte le cose*, ed. A. Bernat Vistarini and J. T. Cull (Alessandria: Edizioni dell'Orso, 2005), question 278, pp. 184–187.

The French saying "*Entre le fromage et la poire...*" is quoted from LeRoux de Lincy, *Le livre des proverbes français* (Paris: Delahays, 1859), p. 198; A. Callot, *Nouveau dictionnaire proverbial, satirique et burlesque, plus complet que ceux qui ont paru jusqu'à ce jour, à l'usage de tout le monde* (Paris, 1826), p. 325: "This expression signifies the end of the meal when everybody starts to feel cheerful and in a mood to laugh"; D'Hautel, *Dictionnaire du cas langage ou des manières de parler usitées parmi les peuples* (Paris: Haussmann, 1808): "*Entre la poire et le fromage on parle de mariage*" (Between the pear and the cheese one speaks of marriage, meaning at that moment one is disposed to gaiety); *Dictionnaire des proverbes français et des façons de parler comiques, burlesques et familières avec l'explication et les étymologies les plus avérées* (Paris, 1758), p. 279.

The quotation from Michelangelo Buonarroti is in *Opere varie* (Florence: Le Monnier, 1863), p. 380.

For the quote from Petrarch, see *Disperse e attribuite*, ed. A. Solerti (Florence: Sansoni), 1909, a. 1374, 213, v. 120.

For the poetry of Pietro Cantarini, see *Le poesie sulla natura delle frutta e i canterini di Firenze* in *Attraveso il Medioevo. Studi e ricerche*, ed.

F. Novati (Bari: Laterza, 1905), pp. 332–335 (the quotation is on p. 333; the italics are mine).

G. Nigro, *Gli uomini dell'Irco. Indagine sui consumi di carne nel basso Medioevo. Prato alla fine del '300* (Florence: Le Monnier, 1983), pp. 167 ff., for the dates of the hotel in Prato.

The notice about the Visconti is in P. C. Decembrio, *Vita di Filippo Maria Visconti*, ed. E. Bartolini (Milan: Adelphi, 1983), LII, pp. 100–101.

The appetite of Morgante and Margutte appears in L. Pulci, *Morgante*, cantare 18, 155, ed. P. Sarrazin (Turnhout: Brepols, 2001).

For the *Capitolo del bacio* by Giovanni Della Casa and the *Capitolo sopra la salsiccia* by Girolamo Ruscelli, see respectively *Il primo libro delle opere burlesche* (pp. 141–142) and *Il secondo libro delle opere burlesche* (pp. 112–116) (Usecht al Reno: Broedelet, 1771), reprinted from the edition by Domenico Giglio (Venice, 1564–66).

The two quotations by A. F. Grazzini are taken from *La Pinzochera*, act 2, scene 5, in *Opere*, vol. 2: *Commedie*, ed. P. Fanfani (Florence: LeMonnier, 1859), pp. 306, 248.

The letter by Francesco de la Arme is quoted by G. Malacarne, *Sulla mensa del principe. Alimentazione e banchetti alla Corte dei Gonzaga* (Modena: Il Bulino, 2000), p. 186.

For the text by Oviedo: *Sommario della naturale e generale istoria dell'Indie occidentali di Gonzalo Ferdinando d'Oviedo*, in G. B. Ramusio, *Navigazioni e viaggi*, ed. M. Milanesi, (Turin: Einaudi, 1985), V, pp. 300–301.

On the centrality of the notion of "the status of foodstuffs" in J.-L. Flandrin's historiographic observation, see M. Montanari, "Un historien gourmand," in *Le désir et le goût. Une autre histoire (XIII^e–XVIII^e siècles)*, ed. O. Redon, L. Sallmann, and S. Steinberg (Saint-Dénis: Presses Universitaires de Vincennes, 2005), pp. 371–381 and pp. 375–378.

## Chapter 3. Peasant Fare

Homer, *Odyssey*, IX, 187 ff, in the Italian translation by M. G. Ciani (Venice: Marsilio, 1994), pp. 305–307.

P. Camporesi writes about "*hippomolgói*" in "Il formaggio maladetto," in *Le Officine dei sensi* (Milan: Garzanti, 1985), p. 59.

On food images of the "barbarity" during the early Middle Ages, see M. Montanari, *La fame e l'abbondanza. Storia dell'alimentazione* (English translation: *The Culture of Food* [Boston: Wiley, 1996]), pp. 9–10, for the ideological opposition between nature and culture.

The quotation by Pliny the Elder comes from Storia naturale, XI, 239, ed. G. B. Conte, (Turin: Einaudi, 1983), II, p. 658: "*Mirum barbaras gentes, quae lacte vivant, ignorare aut spernere tot saeculis casei dotem.*" The one by Columella comes from *L'arte dell'agricultura*, ed. C. Carena (Turin: Einaudi, 1977), VII, 2, 1, p. 498: "*casei lactisque abundantia non solum agrestit satirat, sed etiam elegantium mensas iucundis et numerosis dapibus exornat.*"

See Apicius's treatise in the edition by J. André: *Apicius, l'art culinaire* (Paris: Les Belles Lettres, 1974).

For the bread and cheese of the Brescian peasants: *Le carte del monastero dei santi Cosima e Damiano (Brescia) 1127–1275*, ed. P. Merati (Brescia: Fondazione Civiltà Bresciana, 2005) n. 2, p. 66; n. 30, p. 68; n. 31, p.71; n. 39, p. 86; n. 42, p. 89; n. 58, p. 132, n. 96, p. 199; n. 155, p. 299. For the distribution of bread and meat: n. 72, p. 156.

The prejudices of medical science regarding the healthfulness of cheese are examined in M. Nicoud, "Aux origines d'une médecine préventive: les traités diététique en Italie et en France (XIII–XVᵉ siècles)," doctoral thesis, 3 vols., École Pratique des Hautes Etudes, Paris 1998, IV section, 1, pp. 320–321. See also P. Camporesi, *Il formaggio maledetto*, 52 ff.

On the cliché from the Salerno school that recommends caution in the consumption of cheese: *Regimen sanitatis. Flos medicinae Scholae Salerni*, I, IX, 8:14, p. 122. See I. Naso, *Formaggio del Medioevo. La "Summa lacticiniorum" di Pantaleone da Confienza* (Turin: Il Segnalibro, 1990), p. 72. For listings of proverbs: E. Strauss, *Dictionary of European Proverbs*, (New York: Routledge, 1994), n. 1456; C. Lapucci, *Dizionario dei proverbi italiani* (Milan: Mondadori, 2007), F 1074: "*Ogni formaggio è sano dato da avara mano*"; Boggione and Massobrio, *Dizionario dei proverbi*, v. 1.7.8.18.1: "*Il formaggio è sano se vien da avara mano*"; LeRoux de Lincy, *Le livre des proverbes français* (Paris: Delahays, 1859), p. 198; Sebastiàn de Horozco (1510–1580), *Teatro universal de proverbios*, ed. J. L. Alonso Hernandez (Salamanca, 1986), n. 1027. The quotation by B. Pisanelli is in *Trattato della natura de' cibi e del bere* (Carmagnola: Bellone, 1589), p. 45.

I quoted the interpretation of C. M. Counihan, *Around the Tuscan Table: Food, Family, and Gender in Twentieth-century Florence* (London: Routledge, 2004), p. 41: "The peasants produced and ate little cheese—a fact recognized in the popular Florentine proverb. . . . The proverb also hinted at the age-old struggle between landlords and peasants over the allocation of resources, and the economic truth that peasants had access only to cheap foods that fueled their bodies for work, not high fat foods like cheese, because they owed these to landlords or sold them." Everything that we have seen (and will see in the next chapter) demonstrates the contrary: cheese could be enjoyed by many, but was considered primarily a peasant food, perfectly suited to nourishing the body "for work." In the same vein as Counihan, though less explicit, is the comment by P. Guazzotti and M. F. Oddera, *Il grande dizionario dei proverbi italiani* (Bologna: Zanichelli, 2006), p. 37: "If the peasant has to be satisfied with poor, basic foods, it is better that he not know how good the more refined are. In the countryside, in fact, peasants had to give the better products to the landlords" (on the assumption that both pears and cheese are particularly "refined" foods).

## Chapter 4. When Rustic Food Becomes the Fashion

For the monastic model, see M. Montanari, *Alimentazione e cultura nel Medioevo* (Rome: Laterza, 1988), pp. 63 ff. For the quotation from L. Moulin, see *La vita quotidiana dei monaci nel Medioevo* (Milan: Mondadori, 1988), p. 70. On the position of dairy products in the meat-free diet, see E. Vacandard, *Carême (Jeûne du)*, in *Dictionnaire de Théologie Catholique*, c. 1742; see also A. Capatti and M. Montanari, *La cucina italiana. Storia di una cultura* (Rome: Laterza, 1999), p. 82.

The analyses of B. Laurioux on the role of cheese in medieval European cookbooks appear in the essay "Du bréhémont et d'autres fromages renommés au XVᵉ siècle," in *Scrivere il Medioevo. Lo spazio, la sanità, il cibo. Un libro dedicato a Odile Redon*, ed. B. Larioux and L. Moulinier-Brogi (Rome: Viella, 2001), pp. 331–332. On p. 332, the "mediterraneity" of the taste for cheese is suggested.

The recipe for cheese on a spit is in *Il libro della cucina del sec. XIV*, ed. F. Zambrini (Bologna: Romagnoli, 1863), pp. 66–67.

For the relationship between the diffusion of pasta and the success of cheese, see A. Capatti and M. Montanari, *La cucina italiana*, pp. 63–64. The quotation from Boccaccio obviously comes from the *Decameron*, v. III, 3; see M. Montanari, *La fame e l'abbondanza (The Culture of Food)*, p. 119.

For quotations of the text by Pantaleone da Confienza, see I. Naso, "Summa lacticiniorium," pp. 138–141. See also p. 139 on the opinions of ancient physicians. Pantaleone quotes the work of the Jewish doctor and philosopher, Isaac, who lived in the tenth century, *De dietis particularibus*.

The letter by Gaspare da Verona is quoted by B. Larioux, *Gastronomie, humanisme et société à Rome au milieu de XVᵉ siècle. Autour du "De honesta voluptate" de Platina* (Florence: Sismel/Edizioni del Galuzzo, 2006), p. 305. On p. 323 is the quotation from his biography of Paul II. On p. 317, Petrarch's predilection for "poor foods"; see also E. Fenzi, "Etica, estetica e politica del cibo in Petrarca," *Quaderni d'Italia* XI (2006), pp. 65–95.

The text by A. Beccadelli (*Elogio de caseo*, ed. A. Cinquini, 1910) is available on the Internet site "Poeti d'Italia."

For the use of brie in Italian cookbooks, see *Liber de coquina*, I, 29, ed. L. Sada and V. Valente (Bari: Puglia Grafica Sud, 1995), p. 116. The quoted recipe from *Libro della cucina* also speaks of using "*cascio di bria*," brie cheese.

For the promotion of quality cheeses in the fourteenth and fifteenth centuries, see again B. Laurioux, *Du bréhémont*: in 1343 the lord of Chalencon gave a dozen cheeses from Craponne (his property) to the French chancellor who was passing through Puy (p. 323); in 1430 the municipal authorities of Tours presented bréhémont to counselors of the queen of Sicily (p. 321); the consuls of Saint-Flour offered "gleo" cheese from Alvernia as a Christmas gift to their bishop (p. 326).

For the quotations from fifteenth-century cookbooks, see C. Messisbugo, *Libro nuovo nel qual s'insegna a far d'ogni sorte di vivanda* (Venice: Eredi Giovanni Padovano, 1557), c. 5 (first edition, under the title *Banchetti composizioni de vivande*, Ferrara, 1549); B. Scappi, *Opera*, (Venice: Tramezzino, 1579), passim. On the importance of Scappi in the history of Italian cooking, see A. Capatti and M. Montanari, *La cucina italiana*, pp. 15 ff. See also p. 64 on the long-lasting custom of adding sugar and cinnamon to pasta with cheese.

## Chapter 5. A Hard Road to Ennoblement

The text by E. Bentivoglio can be found in *Le satire et altre rime piacevoli* (Venice, 1557), c. 16r. Ample commentary in P. Camporesi, "Certosini e marzolini. L'iter casearium de Pantaleone da Confienza nell'Europa dei latticini," in *La miniera del mondo. Artieri inventori impostori* (Milan: Il Saggiatore, 1990), pp. 90–96.

*Formaggiata di sere Stentato al serenissimo re della virtude* by Giulio Landi can be found in the edition by A. Capatti (Milan: Comitato per la tutela del formaggio grana padana, 1991); the quotations in the text are on pp. 46, 51–53, 58–59, 63. After the first edition (1542), a second (1575) and a third (1601) appeared, "purged" of various obscenities and sexual allusions contained in the first, in observance of Counterreformation morality.

For the letter by Tolomei to Giulio Landi (April 7, 1545), see *Delle lettere di M. Claudio Tolomei libri sette* (Venice, 1547), p. 118: "For the cheese you are sending me I thank you very much, but I will thank you all the more when it has arrived, and doubtless even more when I have eaten it."

The passages from B. Pisanelli, *Trattato della natura de' cibi e del bere* (Carmagnola: Bellone, 1589), p. 45, and A. Petronio, *Del viver de gli uomini, et di conservar la sanità* (Rome: Domenico Basa, 1592), p. 187, are also discussed in Camporesi, "Il formaggio maledetto," p. 68, and Camporesi, "Certosini e marzolini," p. 89.

The quotation from Angelo Beolco (known as Il Ruzante) is from *La Pastoral. La prima oratione. Una lettera giocosa*, ed. G. Padoan (Padua: Antenore, 1978), p. 418.

The treatise by J. P. Lotichius, *De casei nequitia* (Frankfurt am Main, 1643), from which is quoted c. 5r, "*ad fossores, et proletarios, rejicienda*," was followed a few years later by *Tractatus de Adversatione Casei* by M. Schoockius; see *Tractatus de Butyro* (Gröningen, 1664).

Citations from A. Gatti, *Il formaggio biasmato* (1635, derived from a previous manuscript not earlier than 1598), ed. F. Minonzio (Milan: Comitato per la tutela del formaggio grana padana, 1994), are at pp. 57–58, 69, 74–75.

## Chapter 6. The Ideology of Difference and Strategies of Appropriation

On the ideology of difference and its alimentary implications, see M. Montanari, *La fame e l'abbondanza* (*The Culture of Food*), pp. 109–110, and M. Montanari, "Immagine del contadino e codici di comportamento alimentare," in *Per Vito Fumaglli. Terra, uomini, istituzioni medievali*, ed. M. Montanari and A. Vasino (Bologna: Clueb, 2000), pp. 199–213.

The texts cited are G. Albani, *De sanitatis custodia*, ed. G. Carbonelli (Pinerolo: Tipografia Sociale, 1906); M. Savonarola, *Libreto de tutte le cosse che se magnano. Un'opera di dietetica del sec. XV*, ed. J. Nystedt (Stockholm: Almqvist & Wiksell, 1988); and G. C. Croce, *Le sottilissime astuzie di Bertoldo. Le piacevoli e ridicolose semplicità di Bertoldo*, ed. P. Camporesi (Turin: Einaudi, 1978). The death of Bertoldo is on p. 74 of the last.

The collection of proverbial sayings (with occasional commentary) compiled around the end of the sixteenth century by the Florentine Francesco Serdonati is preserved in a copy in the Biblioteca Medicea Laurenziana of Florence (Codex Laurenziano-Mediceo-Palatino 62, four volumes). The original has been lost. A few notices in F. Brambilla Ageno, "Premessa a un repertorio di frasi proverbiali," in *Studi lessicali*, ed. P. Bongrani, F. Magnani, and D. Trolli (Bologna: Clueb, 2000), p. 402 n. 6 (originally in *Romance Philology* XIII [1960], pp. 242–264). I will make frequent reference in the course of this book to the collection by Serdonati (to which I had access thanks to the collaboration of Francesca Pucci).

The proverb "Whoever is used to turnips . . ." is found in c. 156v of vol. 1.

Elsewhere I have already examined the "strategies of approval" with which the cuisine of elites includes and ennobles humble food: M. Montanari, "Cucina povera, cucina ricca," *Quaderni Medievali* 52 (2001), pp. 95–105 (reprinted with a few changes under the title "La cucina scritta come fonte per lo studio della cucina orale," *Food and History* 1, no. 1 [2003], p. 251–259). See also M. Montanari, *Il cibo come cultura* (Rome: Laterza, 2004; English translation, *Food Is Culture* [New York: Columbia University Press, 2004), pp. 41–49. See pp. 137–142 for the food/language parallelism (extensively examined in the fields of anthropology, linguistics, and semiotics).

For the recipe with brie, see the thirteenth-century *Liber de coquina*, I, 29, ed. L. Sada and V. Valente (Bari: Puglia Grafica Sud, 1995), p. 116.

The letter to Barbara Gonzaga is quoted in G. Malacarne, *Sulla mensa del principe. Alimentazione e banchetti alla Corte dei Gonzaga* (Modena: Il Bulino, 2000), p. 102.

The passage from Columella is cited in the notes to chapter 3.

## Chapter 7. A High-Born Fruit

The quotation from Chrétien de Troyes is in *Erec et Enide*, v. 4240; see the edition with Italian translation by C. Noacco (Milan: Luni, 1999). See J. LeGoff, *Il meraviglioso e il quotidiano nel'Occidente medievale* (Rome: Laterza, 1983), p. 97.

On the importance of preserved food in the alimentary model of the peasantry, see M. Montanari, *Il cibo come cultura* (*Food Is Culture*), pp. 19–22.

The simile of the pear and the gentlewoman is in a text edited by E. Faral, "Des Vilains ou des XXIII manières de Vilains," *Romania* XLVIII (1922), pp. 51–53, cited in H. Braet, "A thing most brutish": The Image of the Rustic in Old French Literature," in *Agriculture in the Middle Ages: Technology, Practice, and Representation*, ed. D. Sweeney (Philadelphia: University of Pennsylvania Press, 1995), p. 198.

For Rurizio's gift, see *Ruritii Epistulae* II, 60 (in *Monumenta Germaniae Historica, Auctores antiquissimi*, VIII, p. 349): "*centum pira sublimitati vestrae, alia centum filiae meae destinare praesumpsi.*" According to Emmanuelle Raga, the large number of fruits would make one think this a gift of quantity rather than quality: "this would therefore not appear to be a prestigious gift"; "La place de l'alimentation dans les rapports sociaux de l'aristocracie gallo-romaine. V<sup>e</sup>–VI<sup>e</sup> siècles," *Mémoire de license en histoire médiévale*, ed. Alain Dierkens (Brussels: Université Libre de Bruxelles, Faculté de Philosophie et Lettres, 2005–6), p. 147. But the social position of the protagonists leads one to believe the contrary.

Charlemagne's instructions on fruit trees are in *Capitulare de villis*, 70 (in *Monumenta Germaniae Historica, Capitularia regum Francorum*, I, n. 32, p. 90).

The "chain of being" (see A. O. Lovejoy, *The Great Chain of Being* [Cambridge, Mass.: Harvard University Press, 1936]) was linked to the alimentary imagination by A. J. Grieco, "The Social Order of Nature and the Natural Order of Society in Late 13th–Early 14th Century Italy," *Miscellanea Mediaevali* 21, no. 2 (1992), pp. 898–907; A. J. Grieco, "Les plantes, les régimes végétariens et la mélancholie à la fin du Moyen Age et au début de la Renaissance italienne," in *Le monde végétal (XIIᵉ–XVIIᵉ siècles). Savoirs et usages sociaux,* ed. A. J. Grieco, O. Redon, and L. Tongiorgi Tomasi (Paris: Presses Universitaires de Vincennes, 1993), pp. 11–29. See M. Montanari, *La fame e l'abbondanza* (*The Culture of Food*), pp. 112–113.

On the "poetry of fruit" by Pietro Cantarini, see chapter 2.

The observation by Pope Paul II is in B. Laurioux, *Gastronomie, humanisme et société à Rome au milieu de XVᵉ siècle. Autour du "De honesta voluptate" de Platina* (Florence: Sismel/Edizioni del Galuzzo, 2006), p. 468. See also p. 290 for Gianantonio Campano's gift and epigram.

The report of the pears sent to Vienna comes from *Dato de cosina, ovvero Conti resi per il Maestro di cucina del Cardinal Cristoforo Madruzzo per il mese di dicembre 1564*, manuscript preserved in the Biblioteca del Commune di Trento, ed. Salvana Chiesa (whom I thank for pointing it out).

B. Andreolli, *Le cacce dei Pico. Pratiche venatorie, paesaggio e società a Mirandola tra Medioevo ed Età moderna* (S. Felice sul Panaro: Gruppo Studi Bassa Modenese, 1988), pp. 66, 68, discussed the gifts of fruit made by the Gonzagas; on the particular importance of pears, see Andreolli, "Dal brolo a frutteto. Alle origini della pericultura nell'Oltrepò mantovano," in *Pera dell'Oltre mantovano. Studio preliminare per l'Indicazione Geografica Protetta*, ed. C. Malagoli (Mantua: Consorzio Pera tipica mantovana, n.d.), pp. 89–106.

For the sonnet by T. Campanella, see *Le poesie*, ed. F. Giancotti (Turin: Einaudi, 1998), p. 566 n. 146. For the text by Ercole Bentivoglio, see chapter 5.

For the information in the text, see G. Soderini, *Il trattato degli arbori*, ed. A. Bacchi della Lega (Bologna: Romagnoli Dall'Acqua, 1904), pp. 522–524.

See M. Montanari, *Il cibo come cultura*, pp. 18–19, for the idea of "extending the time."

A. Gallo, *Le venti giornate dell'agricoltura et de'piaceri della villa* (Venice, 1615), pp. 100 ff. The definitive version of this text, to which I refer, is the final step of a work in progress that began with *Le dieci giornate* (1564) and continued with *Le tredici giornate* (1566).

About the famine of 1338, see Anonimo Romano, *Cronaca*, ed. G. Porta (Milan: Adelphi, 1981), IX, p. 35.

C. Felici, *Dell'insalata e piante che in qualunque modo vengono per cibo del'homo*, ed. G. Arbizzoni (Urbino: QuattroVenti, 1986), p. 92, on the practice of turning dried pears into flour. Columella had already talked about dried pears in *L'arte dell'agricoltura*, 2.21.3.

V. Tanara, *L'economia del cittadino in villa* (Bologna: Monti, 1644, but I quote from the Brigonci edition, Venice, 1655), p. 392, on dried pears, which only exceptionally "are still eaten by city dwellers."

Pears from the land of Cockaigne are in *Storia de Campriano contadino*, ed. A. Zanetti (Bologna: Romagnoli, 1884), p. 61; "*Ci son di Gennar le frutte fresche / belle e mature, e han la camicia rotta / le pere moscatella e gentilesche*" (As of January there is fresh fruit, beautiful and ripe, and skin is bursting on the moscatella and gentilesche pears).

The treatise by Carroli was studied by E. Casali, *Il villano dirozzato. Cultura, società e potere nelle campagne romagnole della Controriforma* (Florence: La Nuova Italia, 1982); quotations in my text are on pp. 290, 294.

Even Agostino Gallo stresses the brief durability of the fruits of the pear tree, above all the most delicate and flavorful: the bergamot variety "is perhaps the most flavorful and delicate of all, but it does not keep for very long" (*Le vinti giornate*, pp. 106–107).

The work by J. B. de la Quintinie, *Instruction pour les jardins fruitiers et potagers* (Arles: Actes Sud, 1999), chap. III, pp. 390–407 on pears was published posthumously in 1690, two years after the death of the author.

On the illustrated catalogue by Bimbi, see *Bartolomeo Bimbi, un pittore de piante e animale alla corte dei Medici*, ed. S. Meloni Trkulja and L. Tongiorgi Tomasi (Florence: Edifir, 1998), pp. 140–141.

The "infatuation with pears" was discussed by F. Quellier, *Des fruits et des hommes. L'arboriculture fruitière en Ile-de-France (vers 1600–1800)* (Rennes: Presses Universitaires, 2003), pp. 65–67; see also Quellier, "Les fruits de la civilité française: l'engouement des élites du XVIIe siècle pour le jardin fruitier-potager," *Polia. Revue de l'art des jardins* VIII (2007), pp. 25–39. On the improvement of species cultivated in the modern era, see Quellier, *La table des Français. Une histoire culturelle (XVe–début XIXe siècles)* (Rennes: Presses Universitaires, 2007), pp. 85–87.

## Chapter 8. When Desire Conflicts with Health

The quotation from Nicolas Venette (*Usage des fruits des arbres, pour se conserver en santé, ou pour se guérir, lors que l'on est malade*, 1683) is in F. Quellier, *La table des Français*, p. 177.

On the relation between gastronomy and diet, the studies by J.-L. Flandrin are numerous and fundamental: see at least "Condamenti, cucina e dietetica tra XIV a XVI secolo," in *Storia dell'alimentazione*, ed. J-L. Flandrin and

M. Montanari (Rome: Laterza, 1997), and for the contested use of fruit, *Chronique de Platine* (Paris: Odile Jacob, 1992), pp. 133, 270.

On the prevalence in the Middle Ages of the *regimen conservativum* (nourishing the body with foods similar to one's nature) with regard to the *regimen reductivum* (nourishing the body with foods in opposition to one's nature, to arrive at a greater equilibrium), see J.-L. Flandrin, "La distinzione attraverso il gusto," in *La vita privata dal Rinascimento all'Illuminismo*, ed. P. Ariès and G. Duby (Rome: Laterza, 2001), pp. 228–229 (with particular reference to the text of Aldobrandino da Siena, *Le régime du corps*, ed. L. Landouzy and R. Pépin [Paris: Champion, 1911], I, 2, p. 13). Flandrin situates the passage of one perspective to the other in the sixteenth century, but I am of the opinion that the supremacy of the first regimen had come to be doubted even earlier. According to the fourteenth-century Piedmontese doctor Giacomo Albini, the *reductivum* (or *preservativum*) regime would be "safer" (*tutior*) than the other. G. Albini, *De sanitatis custodia*, ed. G. Carbonelli (Pinerolo: Tipografia Sociale, 1906), IV, pp. 107–110.

The opinions of the various *auctoritates* (Galen, Avicenna, Averroes, and others) on the nutritional value of pears are assembled in the treatise on edible fruit by Battista Massa (1472), dedicated to Ercole I d'Este. See M. Marighelli, *"De Frustibus vescendis" di Battista Massa da Argenta* (Ferrara: Pragma, 1989), p. 85.

For Aldobrandino da Siena's position, see *Le régime du corps*, p. 147: *"Poires sont froides au premier degré et sèches au second."*

Arnaldo da Villanova, *Regimen Sanitatis ad regem Aragonum*, X, 56 (in *Arnaldi de Villanova Opera medica omnia*, X.1 (Barcelona: Publicacions i edicions de la Universitat de Barcelona, 1996). See J. Cruz Cruz, *Dietetica medieval*, p. 237.

On medieval dietetics, see M. Weiss Adamson, *Medieval Dietetics: Food and Drink in "Regimen Sanitatis" Literature from 800 to 1400* (Frankfurt am Mein: Lang, 1995).

On the *Tacuina sanitatis*, see C. Opsomer, *L'art de vivre en santé. Images et recettes du Moyen Age, Le Tacuinum Sanitatis* (manuscript 1041), Bibliothèque de l'Université de Liège, f. 4r, p. 139.

For the other quotations, see M. Savonarola in *Libreto de tutte le cosse che se magnano. Un'opera di dietetica del sec. XV*, ed. J. Nystedt (Stockholm: Almqvist & Wiksell, 1988), pp. 89–90; C. Durante da Gualdo, *Il tesoro della sanità. Nel qual si insegna il modo di conservar la sanità e prolungar la vita e si tratta della natura dei cibi e dei remedi dei documenti loro*, ed. E. Camillo (Milan: Serra e Riva, 1982), pp. 99–100.

On Francesco Petrarch's passion for fruit and his arguments with doctors on this subject, see E. Fenzi, "Etica, estetica e politica del cibo in Petrarca," *Quaderni d'Italia* XI (2006), pp. 88–92. The text by Sassoli is in *Lettere a Francesco Datini*, ed. C. Guasti (Florence: LeMonnier, 1880), pp. 370–374 (cf. M. Montanari, *Convivio. Storia e cultura dei piaceri della tavola dall'Antichità al Medioevo* [Rome: Laterza, 1989] pp. 458–460 n. 234).

The opinion of Agostino Gallo is in *Le vinti giornate dell'agricoltura e de'piaceri della villa* (Venice, 1569), p. 106.

For Alexander Neckham, I used M. T. Beonio Brocchieri Fumagalli, *Le enciclopedie dell'Occidente medievale* (Turin: Leoscher, 1981), p. 149.

For the rules of the Salerno school regarding the consumption of pears (the importance of eating them with wine and/or cooking them) see *Regimen Sanitatis. Flos medicinae Scholae Salerni*, ed. A. Sinno (Milan: Mursia, 1987), I, IX, 10.2, pp. 138–139.

For the perseverance into the modern era of medieval prescriptions on the consumption of pears, see, for example, Domenico Romoli (sixteenth century), according to whom the heat required to digest pears can be achieved "either through the exercise of running, or wine" (*La singolar dottrina* [Venice, 1560], XI, 134).

The link between proverbial sayings and medical texts of the Salerno school is stressed by F. Loux and P. Richard, *Sagesse du corps. La santé et la maladie dans les proverbes français* (Paris: Maisonneuve et Larose, 1978). On the relation between scientific tradition and popular culture, see above all J.-L. Flandrin, *Condimenti, cucina e dietetica*, p. 393 (from which I have taken French and English proverbs that imply diffidence toward the pear).

The quotation from A. Chesnel and J.-P. Migne in *Dictionnaire de la sagesse populaire, recueil moral d'apophthegmes, axiomes, etc.* (1855), p. 910: "*Si quelquefois tu manges de la poire/ Il faudra le vin apparier . . . / Sans vin, la poire est poison et venin / Mais si la poire est un fruit non bénin / Aux maudissons le poirier j'abandonne.*" An example of the present-day persistence of these proverbs can be found in G. Cosson, *Inventaire des dictons des terroirs de France* (Paris: Larousse, 2006), p. 293: "*Sur la poire / Le prêtre ou le boire.*"

The Italian proverb that compares the fig (to be eaten with water) to the pear (to be eaten with wine) can be found in many reference works: Boggione and Massobrio, *Dizionario dei proverbi*, v. 1.7.20.5.a; Lapucci, *Dizionario dei proverbi italiani*, F 736; Antoniazzi and Citti, *I detti del mangiare*, n. 1226 (Tuscany); n. 582 (Lombardy); see n. 195 for the variant with peaches.

For the quotation from Hildegard of Bingen, see *Subtilitatum diversarum naturarum creaturarum libri novem*, III, 2 (in *Patrologia Latina*, 197, c. 1218).

Proverbs on boiled pears in F. Loux and P. Richard, *Sagesse du corps*, p. 69 (see G. Cosson, *Inventaire*, p. 293); A. Chesnel and J.-P. Migne, *Dictionnaire*, p. 910: "*Un antidote est en la poire cuite / Sans la cuisson le contraire s'ensuit.*"

For the quotations that follow, see Durante da Gualdo, *Il tesoro della sanità*, p. 109; G. Soderini, *Il trattato degli arbori*, pp. 531, 534; M. Savonarola, *Libretto*, pp. 89–90; G. Simeoni, *De conservanda sanitate. I consigli di un medico del Quattrocento*, ed. M. D'Angelo (Cassacco: Libraria, 1994), p. 77: "*coctis, id est assis in igne, raro uti po[s]sit post cibum cum modico coriandri aut anisi aut feniculi*"; G. B. Fiera, *Coena. Delle virtù delle erbe e quella parte dell'Arte medica che consiste nella regola del vitto*, ed. M. G. Fiorini (Mantua: Galassi, 1992), p. 101 (the first edition of the work was in 1490).

The association cheese/pears in dietetics is in Durante da Gualdo, *Il tesoro della sanità*, p. 153; B. Pisanelli, *Trattato della natura de'cibi e del bere* (Carmagnola: Bellone, 1589), p. 45. The equilibrium between the two foods functions on the axis hot/cold. Less significant in this case would seem to be the opposition moist/dry, because aged cheese is known to have the same dry nature as the pear. Instead, fresh cheese, of a cold and moist nature, not having been dried by salting, is the cheese of choice at the beginning of a meal. For this distinction, see B. Platina, *Il piacere onesto e la buona salute*, ed. E. Faccioli (Turin: Einaudi, 1985), II, 39, p. 51.

For the final quotation by E. Bentivoglio, *Le satire et altre rime piacevoli* (Venice, 1557), c.17r, I used P. Camporesi, "Certosini e marzolini," p. 97. According to Camporesi, the advice of Ercole Bentivoglio would have gone nowhere since there is no trace of cheese among the fruits served at upper-class tables at that time. "The famous, proverbial pairing of cheese and fruit may not yet have come into use or, if it made its way through Italy, it would have to have been primarily where the merchant middle class, particularly in Tuscany and central Italy, maintained close and avaricious sharecropping relations with the peasantry, precisely from whom one had to conceal the pleasure of a pear accompanied by a chunk of cheese." Our interpretive itinerary is clearly going in another direction.

## Chapter 9. Peasants and Knights

*Le dieci tavole dei proverbi*, ed. M. Cortellazzo (Vicenza: Neri Pozza, 1995); the proverb quoted in the text is on p. 71, n. 800. The perseverance of the proverb into the nineteenth century is documented in *Raccolta di proverbi toscani con illustrazioni cavata dai manoscritti di Giuseppe Giusti ed ora ampliata e ordinata* (Florence: LeMonnier, 1853), p. 306, and in the next edition: *Raccolta di proverbi toscani nuovamente ampliate da quella di Giuseppe Giusti*, ed.

G. Capponi (Florence: LeMonnier, 1871). In recent anthologies: C. Lapucci, *Dizionario dei proverbi italiani* (Milan: Mondadori, 2007), F 1072, p. 588. See Antoniazzi and Citti, *I detti del mangiare*, in which the proverb is documented in the Venetian dialect, absolutely identical to the sixteenth-century version: *"Formagio, pero e pan: pasto da vilan; formagio, pan e pero, pasto da cavaliero"* (n. 1409).

For the Spanish proverb, see H. Nuñez and L. De Leon, *Refranes o proverbios en castellano*, 1555, II, 1147, quoted in *Thesaurus proverbiorum Medii Aevi. Lexicon der Sprichwörter des romanisch-germanischen Mittelalters*, ed. S. Singer (Berlin: Walter de Gruyter, 1998), 6, p. 439.

For the French proverb: *Dictionnaire des proverbes français et des façons de parler comiques, burlesques et familières avec l'explication et les étymologies les plus avérées* (Paris, 1758), p. 279. The same as in A. Caillot, *Nouveau dictionnaire proverbial, satirique et burlesque, plus complet que ceux qui ont paru jusqu'à ce jour, à l'usage de tout le monde* (Paris, 1826), p. 325.

For the "separate" circulation of the two parts of the proverb, see Lapucci, *Dizionario*, p. 588: "Even singly the first or the second part has been diffused." (See also the comment quoted in the text.) A few examples are in *I detti del mangiare*: no. 1722: "*Vino, formaggio e pere: pasto da cavaliere*" (with the interesting substitution of wine for bread); no. 889: "*pane, formaggiu e pere: mangiare da cavaliere*" (Puglia).

The opinions of F. Loux and P. Richard are in *Sagesse du corps*, pp. 72–77.

The text by B. Tacconi, *La Danae* (1496), was published by Azzoguidi (Bologna, 1888); the passage quoted is on p. 11.

The proverb about the walnuts is in F. Serdonati, 3, c. 220v. In recent anthologies: V. Boggione and L. Massobrio, *Dizionario dei proverbi*, v. 1.7.7.28.II: "*Noci e pane, pasto da villano; pane e noci, pasto da spose.*" The variant with the dog in place of the peasant is in *Detti del mangiare*, n. 302 (Emilia). Lapucci, *Dizionario dei proverbi*, n. 396, p. 1019, proposes a dietetic explanation: "This means that by eating a moderate amount of walnuts with bread (bread accompanied by walnuts) one obtains a tasty and nutritious dish, worthy of a festive table; by eating many walnuts and little bread one provokes an indigestion."

F. Serdonati lists the two versions of the proverb under C for "*cacio*" and F for "*formaggio*" (2, c.237r). The quotation from Dante comes from *Paradiso*, XV, verses 97 ff.

The quotations that follow come from "Proverbi italiani. Raccolti, e ridotti sotto a certi capi e luoghi comuni per ordine d'alfabeto da Orlando Pescetti," in Vinetia, Appresso Sebastiano Combi (1611), c. 46v; G. C. Croce, *Selva di esperienza nella quale si sentono mille, e tanti Proverbi, provati et esperimentati da' nostri Antichi. Tirato per via d'alfabeto da Giulio Cesare Croce* (Bologna:

Bartolomeo Cochi, 1618); no. 538 in the attributed numbering in G. C. Croce, *L'Eccellenza e Trionfo del Porco e altre opere in prosa*, ed. M. Rouch (Bologna: Pendragon, 2006), p. 176; F. Lena, *Proverbi italiani e latini raccolti già da Francesco Lena . . . et in questa seconda edizione corretti et accresciuti dallo stesso autore* (Bologna: Longhi, 1694), p. 67 (the first edition was published in Lucca in 1674).

In current anthologies only the ambiguous form is listed, which I would consider the oldest. The "simplified" variant has been retained instead in the oral tradition: *"Caciu, pira e pani unn'è cibbu di viddani"* (documented by Ponino De Blasi, Sicily, March 2007).

The greengrocer who sells pears in the city is in Sabadino Degli Arienti, *Le Porretane*, ed. G. Gambarin (Bari: Laterza, 1914), XXXIX, p. 234.

The last quotations are in Petrus de Crescentiis, *Ruralia commoda*, V. 20, ed. W. Richter (Heidelberg: Universitätsverlag C. Winter, 1996), II, p. 153; C. Felici, *Dell'insalata e piante che in qualunque modo vengono per cibo del'homo*, ed. G. Arbizzoni (Urbino: QuattroVenti, 1986), p. 91.

## Chapter 10. To Savor (To Know) / Taste (Good Taste)

For Aldobrandino da Siena's reference to the authority of Avicenna: *Le régime du corps*, eds. L. Landouzy and R. Pépin (Paris: Champion, 1911), 1, 2, p. 14; *"car, si com dist Avicennes, se li cors de l'oume est sains, totes les coses ki li ont millor savour à la bouche, mieux le nourissent."*

The quotation by Maynus de Mayneriis is from *Regimen Sanitatis*, III, 20: *"per condimenta gustui efficiuntur delectabiliora, et per consequens digestibiliora. Nam quod est delectabilis est ad digestionem melius: tum quia per condimenta additur bonitas, et corrigitur malicia"* (from the Lyon edition of 1517, f. 44v).

On the equivalence of goodness and health (good flavor equals good dietetics), see Y. Grappe, *Sulle tracce del gusto. Storia e cultura del vino nel Medioevo* (Rome-Bari: Laterza, 2006), pp. 78–82; F. Pucci Donati, "Dietetica e cucina nel Regimen Sanitatis di Maino de' Maineri," *Food and History* 4, no. 1 (2007), p. 130.

On the equivalence of goodness and health (gustatory goodness equals dietary goodness) in medieval culture, see again Y. Grappe, *Sulle tracce del gusto*, pp. 57–84; M. Montanari, "Sapore e sapere: il senso del gusto come strumento di conoscenza," in *I cinque sensi (per tacer del sesto)*, ed. F. Ghelli (Florence: Le Monnier, 2007), pp. 71–78. The superiority of taste over the other senses as a means of understanding reality is upheld in the thirteenth century by the anonymous *Tractatus de quinque sensibus sed specialiter de saporibus* (or *Summa de saporibus*) studied and published by C. Burnett in "The Superiority of Taste," *Journal of the Warburg and Courtauld Institutes* LIV (1991), pp. 230–238.

For the text by Bentivoglio, see chapter 8.

The passage from Montaigne is in "Apologie de Raymond Sebon": "*C'est à l'aventure quelque sens particulier . . . qui apprend . . . aux frelons, aux fourmis et aux rats, de choisir toujours le meilleur fromage et la meilleure poire avant que d'y avoir tâté*" (*Les Essais*, II, 12).

The *Dialogus Salomonis et Marcolphi* (from which I quote the prologue of part I) can be found in the Camporesi edition of G.C. Croce, *Le sottilissime astuzie di Bertoldo. Le piacevoli e ridicolose semplicità di Bertoldino* (Turin: Einaudi, 1978), p. 170.

On the peasant as a "human beast," see P. Camporesi, *La maschera di Bertoldo. G. C. Croce e la letteratura carnevalesca* (Turin: Einaudi, 1976), pp. 31 ff.

The comment by Landi is in *La Formaggiata di sere Stentato al serenissimo re della virtude*, ed. A. Capatti (Milan: Comitato per la tutela del formaggio gran padano, 1991), p. 52.

The proverb about pears that end up with pigs can be found in Boggione and Massobrio, *Dizionario dei proverbi*, VIII.1.2.3I–II–II.

On the birth (or rather, on the increase in importance) of the idea of "good taste" in the modern era, I referred primarily to J.-L. Flandrin, "La distinzione attraverso il gusto," in *La vita privata dal Rinascimento all'Illuminismo*, eds. P. Ariès and G. Duby (Rome: Laterza, 2001), pp. 230–238, and to L. Vercelloni, *Viaggio intorno al gusto. L'odissea occidentale dalla società di corte all'edonismo di massa* (Milan: Mimesis, 2005), pp. 20–25, 56–59. For the quotation from Voltaire, see under "Goût" in *Encyclopédie ou dictionnaire raisonné des sciences, des arts et des métiers*, v. VII. On the transformation of the idea of "taste" into that of "good taste," see also P. D'Angelo, "Il gusto in Italia e Spagna dal Quattrocento al Settecento," in *Il gusto. Storia di un'idea estetica*, ed. L. Russo (Palermo: Aesthetica, 2000), pp. 11–34; N. Perullo, "Per un'estetica del cibo," *Aesthetica* 78 (2006), pp. 16–17.

A. Hauser, *Storia sociale dell'arte* (Turin: Einaudi, 1998), II, p. 49.

The two stories about Cosimo de'Medici are in A. Poliziano, *Detti piacevoli*, 45, ed. T. Zanat (Rome: Istituto dell'Enciclopedia Italiana, 1983), p. 51; and T. Costo, *Il fuggilozio*, III, 37, ed. C. Calenda (Rome: Salerno, 1989), pp. 199–200.

On Bertoldo's "wild fruits," see chapter 6.

The Catalan proverb is in *Diccionari Català-Valencià-Balear*, ed. A. Alcover (Palma de Mallorca, 1979), VIII, p. 444 (see "Pera").

Sermini's invective against the rustic is included in a series of verses interspersed among his stories: G. Sermini, *Le novelle*, ed. G. Vettori (Rome: Avanzini e Torraca, 1968), 2, p. 600.

For the *Capitolo sulle pesche* (before August 1522) see F. Berni, *Rime*, ed. G. Bàrberi Squarotti (Turin: Einaudi, 1969), pp. 27–30 (the quotations from verses 16–17, 51, 52, 55). Of these verses and the "mystery" to which they allude, I have proposed a literal interpretation, perhaps questionable in an expressive context such as that of Berni's, permeated with metaphors, innuendoes, and allusions (for the most part to practical things or sexual preferences); it is evident in any case that each play on words presupposes a blending of "real" images, which makes the twists of meaning all the more effective.

*Ricordo d'agricoltura* by C. Tarello can be read in the edition by M. Berengo (Turin: Einaudi, 1975); the passage quoted is on p. 122. The first edition of *Ricordo* was published in 1567 in Venice by Rampazzetto. Scottoni's notes are in the eighteenth-century reissue: *Ricordo d'agricoltura di M. Camillo Tarello, corretto, illustrato, aumentato con note, aggiunti e tavole del padre maestro Gian Francesco Scottoni min. conventuale* (Venice: Giammaria Bassaglia, 1772), pp. 245–246.

## Chapter 11. How a Proverb Is Born

The chapter on cardoons (from which I quote verses 16–18) is in F. Berni, *Rime*, ed. G. Bàrberi Squarotti (Turin: Einaudi, 1969), pp. 23–26.

The proverb "May you never know, knave . . ." appears twice in F. Serdonati, 1, c. 106r (with comment quoted in the text): 2, c.237r.

On the birth of a rural elite in the last centuries of the Middle Ages and its progressive decline in the ensuing centuries, see G. Pinto, "Bourgeoisie de village et différenciations sociales dans les campagnes de l'Italie communale (XIIIe–XVe siècles)," in *Les élites rurales dans l'Europe médievale et moderne*, ed. F. Menant and J.-P. Jessenne (Toulouse: Presses Universitaires du Mirail, 2007), pp. 91–110.

The text by the anonymous thirteenth-century Genoese can be read in N. Lagomaggiore, "Rime genovesi dei secoli XIII–XIV," *Archivio glottologico italiano* II (1875–76), p. 280: "*E no so cossa pu dura / ni de maor prosperitae / como vilan chi de bassura / monta en gran prosperitae / otra moo desnatura / pin de orgoio e de peccae.*"

The Calabrese proverb is in *Detti del mangiare*, p. 94.

The proverbial opposition between urban courtesy and peasant knavery is in F. Serdonati, 1, c. 19v.

On the satire of the rustic, see also D. Merlini, *Saggio di ricerche sulla satira contro il villano, con appendice di documenti inediti* (Turin: Loescher, 1894), whose content has been superseded but remains a formidable mine of texts. My own brief examination of *La satira del villano fra imperialismi cittadino e integrazione culturale* is in *La Costruzione del dominio cittadino sulle campagne. Italia centro-settentrionale, secoli XIII–XIV*, ed. Roberta Mucciarelli, Gabriela Piccini, and Giuliano Pinto (Siena: Protagon, 2009), pp. 697–705.

The text by Carroli is in E. Casali, *Il villano dirozzato. Cultura società e potere nelle campagne romagnole della Controriforma* (Florence: La Nuova Italia, 1982), p. 128.

The catalogue of "abuses and vices of peasants" is in the appendix to G. C. Croce, *Le sottilissime astuzie di Bertoldo. Le piacevoli e ridicolose semplicità di Bertoldino* (Turin: Einaudi, 1978), p. 233. Ibid, p. 11, note 5, quotation by Croce taken from *Avvisi burleschi venuto da diverse parti del mondo. Cose notabilissime e degne da essere intese* (Bologna: Cochi, 1628), c. 3v.

Sabadino degli Arienti, *Le Porretane*, ed. G. Gambarin (Bari: Laterza, 1914), XXXVIII, p. 227–229.

On the "chain of being," see chapter 7.

On the image of the peasant/thief that developed in the Italian urban culture of the late Middle Ages and early modern era, see E. Sereni, "Agricoltura e mondo rurale," in *Storia d'Italia. I caratteri originali* (Turin: Einaudi, 1972), I, p. 194. See also G. Cherubini, *L'Italia rurale del basso Medioevo* (Rome: Laterza, 1996), p. 135; G. Piccinni, "Seminare, fruttare, raccogliere," in *Mezzadria e salariati nelle terre di Monte Oliveto Maggiore (1374–1430)* (Milan: Feltrinelli, 1982), pp. 220–221.

On peasant thefts, I have quoted G. Giorgetti, *Contadini e proprietari nell'Italia moderna: rapporti di produzione e contratti agrari dal secolo XVI a oggi* (Turin: Einaudi, 1974), p. 42; M. Rouch, *Les communautés rurales de la campagne bolonaise et l'image du paysan dans l'oeuvre de Giulio Cesare Croce (1550–1609)* (Bordeaux: Presses Universitaires de Bordeaux, 1984), II, pp. 744–745. For France, see Quellier, *La table des Français*, p. 150. Quellier, in *Des fruits et les hommes*, pp. 391–392, has insisted on the symbolic meaning of the thefts in the orchards/gardens.

The proverb on the avarice of the peasant is in Serdonati, 3, c. 6v–7r. "To eat cheese, pears, and bread . . . the peasant would sell the farm" is in O. Pescetti, *Proverbi italiani. Raccolti e ridotti sotto a certi capi e luoghi comuni per ordine alfabetico da Orlando Pescetti* (Venice: Appresso Sebastiano Combi, 1611), c. 46v: "The peasant would sell the farm to eat cheese, bread, and pears." For nineteenth-century versions, see *Raccolta di proverbi toscani*, p. 306, and F. Bellonzi, *Proverbi toscani* (Florence: Giunti, 2000), p. 31, n. 421.

The quotation from Landi in *Formaggiata di sere Stentato al serenissimo re della virtude*, p. 54. Also in Pescetti, *Proverbi italiani*, c, 46v: "*Il villano venderia il gaban per mangiar cacio, pere e pan*" (the peasant would sell his clothes to eat cheese, pears, and bread). The proverb also exists in a French variant, of likely Italian origin: *"Si le paysan savait ce qu'est manger fromage, poire et pain, il engagerait son cheval pour en manger toute l'année"* (if the peasant knew what it is to eat cheese, pears, and bread, he would pawn his horse to eat them all year round). The proverb is listed at www.culture.gouv.fr/public/mistral/proverbe.fr.

A modern version of the proverb stresses the moral aspect (condemnation of gluttony) while overlooking the social figure of the peasant: *"Il goloso venderà casa e averi per mangiare formaggio, pane e pere"* (the glutton will sell house and possessions to eat cheese, bread, and pears).

*"Al villan, che mai si sazia non gli far torto, ne grazia"* is documented in Pescetti, *Proverbi italiani*, c. 237v.

Crescenzi's remark is in *Ruralia commoda*, XI, 9, ed. W. Richter (Heidelberg: Universitätsverlag C. Winter, 1998), p. 215.

## Chapter 12. "Do Not Share Pears with Your Master": The Proverb as the Site of Class Conflict

The reproach made by the king to Bertoldo is in G. C. Croce, *Le sottilissime astuzie di Bertoldo*, p. 43.

For the diffusion of the proverb on the division of pears in Spain and France, see *Thesaurus proverbiorum Medii Aevi. Lexicon der Sprichwörter des romanisch-germanischen Mittelalters*, ed. S. Singer (Berlin: Walter de Gruyter, 1998), 6, 7, 2, 3, 2, 2, p. 53. For the versions quoted in the text, see J. Morawski, *Proverbes français antérieurs au XV^e siècle* (Paris: Champion, 1925), 2058: *"Qui o seignor part poires il n'a pas des plus belles"* (whoever shares pears with his master does not get the best); Lapucci, *Dizionario dei proverbi italiani*, M 575.

Sebastiàn de Horozco, *Teatro universal de proverbios*, ed. J. L. Alonso Hernandez (Gröningen/Salamanca, 1986), n. 1065, documents the use already in the sixteenth century of the Spanish proverb, *"En burlas ni en veras / con su señor non partas peras."* The same is found in Francisco de Espinosa, *Refranero (1527–1547)*, ed. E. S. O'Kane (Madrid: Imprenta Aguirre, 1968), p. 187. For the present-day use of the proverb, see E. Strauss, *Dictionary of European Proverbs* (London: Routledge, 1994), 1556. The interpretation concerning respect can be found in www.members.fortunecity.com/flopezr/html/espanol/libros/a/refranes.htm: *"Ni en burlas, ni en veras, con tu amo* [i.e., señor] *partas peras.* Advierte el respeto con que siempre debe tratarse a los superiores."* For the variant of hard pears: usuarios.lycos.es/sequeros/refranes/refranes.htm. In Catalan also: *"Ni de burles ne de veres, amb ton senyor ni vulguis partir peres"* (with your master do not risk dividing pears: he will eat the ripe ones, you the sour ones).

The comment of R. Cotgrave in *Dictionarie of the French and English tongues* (London 1611) is apt: "He that eates peares with his Lord either cannot, or should not pick such as he likes" (quoted by T. Scully in the repertory of French and English proverbs in "Comme lard es pois," 82).

The proverb about the bear is listed in Lapucci, *Dizionario dei proverbi*, o 567, p. 1075, who rightly remarks: "He who has business with someone more powerful and arrogant risks losing everything he has invested."

For the simile of *potentes* (the powerful) with wild animals and bears in particular, see Montanari, *La fame e l'abbondanza* (*The Culture of Food*), p. 38.

The expression *fiumane di proverbi*, "streams of proverbs," is used by Camporesi in his introduction to G. C. Croce, *Le sottilissime astuzie de Bertoldo*, p. 38.

For the definition of the proverb as "maximally polyvalent," see M. Rouch, *Les communautés rurales*, II, p. 994.

From E. Schulze-Busacker I have used "Eléments de culture populaire dans la littérature courtoise," in *La culture populaire au Moyen Age*, ed. P. Boglioni (Montreal: Les Editions Univers, 1979), pp. 81–100 (on p. 100 is the observation that recourse to proverbs serves "less to single out a class or a particular way of perceiving the world . . . than to create a distance, to depersonalize the discourse"); and *Proverbes et expressions proverbiales dans la littérature narrative du Moyen Age français* (Geneva: Slatkine, 1985), pp. 15–16.

Other references are in A. J. Greimas, "Idiotismes, proverbes, dictons," *Cahiers de Lexicologie* II (1960), pp. 41–61, and S. Schmarje, *Das sprichwörtliche Material in den Essais von Montaigne* (Berlin: De Gruyter, 1973).

For the discussion of marginal iconography, see L. Randall, *Images in the Margins of Gothic Manuscripts* (Berkeley: University of California Press, 1966); M. Camille, *Image on the Edge*; A. Otwell, "Medieval Manuscript Marginalia and Proverbs" (www.heyotwell.com/work/arthistory/marginalia.html).

That proverbial texts require a context to have meaning (and that they lose it when taken out of their context, as, for example, in the "anthologies" compiled by scholars or writers) is stressed, for reasons not of a semiotic or linguistic nature, but of an epistemological nature, by S. Shapin, "Proverbial Economies: How an Understanding of Some Linguistic and Social Features of Common Sense Can Throw Light on More Prestigious Bodies of Knowledge, Science for Example," *Social Studies of Science* 31, no. 5 (October 2001), pp. 753–754.

Considerations by N. Zemon Davis on the role of proverbs in the cultural dynamic between upper and lower classes are in *Le culture del popolo*, pp. 312–313.

On *proverbes au vilain*, see A. Tobler, *Li proverbe au vilain. Die Sprichwörter des gemeinen Mannes altfranzösiche Dichtung* (Leipzig, 1895); J. Bednar, "Li proverbe au vilain," *Cahiers d'histoire* II (2000); E. Schulze-Busacker, Les "proverbes au vilain," in *Proverbium: Yearbook of International Proverb Scholarship*, VI (1989), pp. 113–127.

For the "common proverb" by Pisanelli, see chapter 3.

The proverb about the swallow, certainly patterned after Aesop's fable "The Young Man and the Swallow," appears in the *Nicomachean Ethics* by Aristotle (1098a 18) and later enters the collection of proverbs by Zenobius (v.12). See *I proverbi greci. Le raccolte di Zenobio a Diogeniano*, ed. E. Letti (Soverio Manelli: Rubettino, 2006), p. 191, and p. 444 n. 461.

The circularity of knowledge is at the heart of many works by Carlo Ginzburg, among which I particularly recall *Il formaggio e i vermi. Il cosmo di un mugnaio del '500* (Turin: Einaudi, 1976).

I have already quoted *Raccolta di proverbi toscano con illustrazioni cavata da manoscritti di Giuseppe Giusti ed ora ampliata e ordinata* (Florence: Le Monnier, 1853, 1871).

D. Provenzal, *Perchè si dice così?* (Milan: Hoepli, 1958), p. 6.

For the quotation from Bruna Lancia, see Antoniazzi and Citti, *I detti del mangiare*, p. 22.

The proverb that is "turned around," which suggests that the secret not be revealed to the master, can be found only in more recent anthologies; see Guazzotti and Oddera, *Il grande dizionario dei proverbi italiani*, p. 44. I have more than once heard this version myself in various circumstances. One instance was reported by Luca Vaschetti of a peasant grandmother, aged eighty-two, from Ternavasso di Poirino in the province of Torino: "*Il paysan douv nen fe savei quant alè bun il furmag cun i prus*" (the peasant should not know how good is cheese with pears), 2007.

The version that I have called "vengeful and liberating" was brought to my attention by Gabriella Piccinni, who heard it in the house of her grandmother, Nella Monti, in the Sienese countryside.

I have quoted from *Don Quixote* in the Italian translation, by Vittorio Bodini (Turin: Einaudi, 1957).

# Index